WITHDRAWN
UTSA LIBRARIES

The Dynamics of Deterrence

The
DYNAMICS
D of eterrence

Frank C. Zagare

The University of Chicago Press

Chicago and London

FRANK C. ZAGARE is assistant professor of political science at Boston University and is the author of *Game Theory: Concepts and Applications*.

The University of Chicago Press, Chicago 60637
The University of Chicago Press, Ltd., London

Library of Congress Cataloging-in-Publication Data

Zagare, Frank C.
    The dynamics of deterrence.

    Bibliography: p.
    Includes index.
    1. International relations—Research.   2. Nuclear
disarmament.   3. Deterrence (Strategy).   I. Title.
JX1291.Z34   1987   327'.072   86-7037
ISBN 0-226-97763-3

TO TISH

This one's for you.

Contents

Figures and Tables

TABLES

Acknowledgments

This book has had a long gestation period. Along the way, many people have helped. I would like to acknowledge their assistance.

First, Steven J. Brams has been the source for many of the underlying ideas that I develop in this book, and has graciously provided me with specific comments on the entire manuscript. I owe him an enormous debt. D. Marc Kilgour has also been a source of inspiration and useful criticisms. Marc's help has been invaluable. Without a doubt, his comments have helped me improve this work. Jacek Kugler has served as my alter ego on this project. In fact, Jacek believed in the merits of this endeavor before I did. Were it not for his encouragement and suggestions, I would not have finished it. Bruce Bueno de Mesquita, Joseph J. Houska, Randolph M. Siverson, and John M. Rothgeb, Jr., have also helped me, each in his own way. I would like to think that all of the above would be willing to share some of the blame for any shortcomings in the manuscript. I am, however, solely responsible for the way I have taken their advice.

I would also like to thank my family for their love and support: my mother, Jen, and my father, Dom, who have been with me every step of the way; my children, Catherine, Ann, and Elizabeth, who provided me with a unique perspective on the dynamics of deterrence; and my wife, Patty, my silent partner in this entire endeavor, to whom I dedicate this volume.

Introduction

No single concept has dominated the strategic field over the past forty years as has the concept of deterrence. Yet, curiously, the theory of deterrence remains woefully underspecified. Although several classic studies in each of the three "waves" of the deterrence literature identified by Jervis (1979) can be pointed to, no single authoritative source, no seminal work, currently exists. Moreover, the field is literally strewn with a mass of disconnected and seemingly contradictory hypotheses, all purportedly deduced from a common set of assumptions (for a partial listing, see Smith 1982). To appreciate the disarray of this field of study one need only reflect on the nature of the debate in the United States in the late 1960s and the early 1970s over the development of an antiballistic missile system, or the current controversies surrounding the deployment of the MX missile and the Strategic Defense Initiative, or Star Wars, program of the Reagan administration.

The huge gulf that separates proponents and opponents on these and related issues reflects the shaky foundation upon which the theoretical edifice of deterrence theory rests. Inexplicably, the underpinnings of deterrence theory have been more or less ignored since the early 1960s with the demise of American nuclear superiority and the "second wave" of theorizing associated with it. Alas, as I will argue later, a reexamination of this foundation reveals several faults and cracks in the underlying architecture. If deterrence were a building, it would probably be condemned.[1]

---

1. Much the same could also be said for deterrence's intellectual cousin, the bal-

My purpose is to lay a new foundation for the theory of deterrence. This is, of course, a very ambitious goal and I do not claim to present anything more than the blueprint and some initial spadework. Yet, if the proposed new foundation is sounder than the old one, others may be able to make the required structural alterations and additions so that the house of deterrence can be put in order.

To some, the outward appearance of the new structure I propose to build, and the tools that I will use to construct it, will not appear unusual. The rational-choice approach in general, and game theory in particular, has long been part of the deterrence landscape. Indeed, much of the original foundation of the theory was laid by workers such as Schelling (1960, 1966), Ellsberg (1959, 1961), Kaplan (1958), Snyder (1961, 1972), Kahn (1960, 1962, 1965), Morgenstern (1959), and Rapoport (1964), who labored at least partly in this tradition.

Although the outward appearance of this structure may seem familiar, the inner "dynamics" are not. The methodology I plan to use—called the theory of moves—departs in several significant ways from traditional game-theoretic models. These differences, as I hope to demonstrate, make this new methodology particularly suited for examining the deterrence relationship and for overcoming some of the more glaring deficiencies of deterrence theory in its current manifestation.

In recasting deterrence theory, I shall proceed as follows: In chapter 1, a fundamental limitation of the theory, as it is presently formulated, will be discussed and the inability of several extant methodologies to overcome this problem demonstrated. In chapter 2, I will use the theory of moves to construct a new model of mutual deterrence. In chapter 3, this model will be extended to deterrence in its unilateral variant. Chapter 4 will explore the complications introduced into the deterrence relationship by power asymmetries and the lack of

---

ance of power. For a trenchant critique, and the need to place this theory on a firmer theoretical footing, see Wagner (1984).

a capable retaliatory threat. In chapter 5, I will apply the model developed in the previous chapters to three games played during the 1967 Six-Day War and show that the theoretical framework presented herein offers a more satisfying explanation of these games than competing methodologies. Chapter 6 will use this framework to offer an evaluation of President Nixon's decision to place American strategic forces on a worldwide alert during the 1973 war in the Middle East. Similarly, in chapter 7, the strategic relationship of the superpowers will be scrutinized in light of the deductions of chapters 2, 3, and 4. Some final thoughts are collected in the epilogue that follows chapter 7.

Before going any further, however, I would like to dispel, in advance, some possible misunderstandings about both the nature of the model I construct and the methodology I develop in this book. First of all, the notion of deterrence that I bring to bear in this work is rather catholic. While I start out by focusing on adversarial, interstate relationships, I do not mean to suggest that deterrence is restricted to only this kind of interaction. Indeed, in chapter 5, in examining two games played just prior to the 1967 war in the Middle East, I argue that the United States sought to deter Israel from taking certain actions that would precipitate a war in the area. In my opinion, the model elaborated in Part I is as appropriate for analyzing deterrence games played between allies as it is for analyzing deterrence games played between hostile states.

By focusing exclusively on deterrence at the interstate level, I also do not mean to suggest that deterrence relationships are unique to international affairs. As others have pointed out (e.g., Williams 1975, 68), deterrence operates at multiple levels and in diverse settings. It frequently plays an important role in husband-wife, parent-child, employer-employee, and state-citizen relationships, to name just a few. Because the model that I build in this book is completely general, it can also be used to study the other kinds of deterrence games that we are all so familiar with.

Finally, I would like to emphasize that the particular methodology that I employ and extend in this work is also potentially applicable to a wide variety of social settings beyond the immediate area of deterrence, broadly defined. As should become evident, since the theory of moves framework is not content-specific, it may easily be used to model any number of conflict-of-interest situations. In fact, many of the concepts associated with this framework were first developed to probe the nature of "superior beings" (Brams 1983)! For this reason, it is my hope that this work will be of interest to social scientists whose interests are not necessarily confined to strategic issues and national security affairs.

Part I

Toward a Reformulation of the Theory of Deterrence

1

The Problem with Deterrence Theory

"In its simplest form, deterrence . . . is basically an attempt by party A to prevent party B from undertaking a course of action which A regards as undesirable, by threatening to inflict unacceptable costs upon B in the event that the action is taken" (Williams 1975, 67). This definition of deterrence, distilled from a reading of leading theorists of nuclear strategy, sets forth both the ends and means of deterrence. The theory of deterrence, however, involves much more than an exercise in definition. It is safe to say that the bulk of deterrence theory has been focused on delineating the conditions under which deterrence will succeed. Unfortunately as Patrick Morgan (1983, 15) has rightly observed, "as it stands, deterrence theory does not really do this."

Significantly, the inability of deterrence theory to provide an answer to such a fundamental question is not due only to the lack of analytic certainty, as Freedman (1981, 182) suggests. The problem with the theory lies much deeper than this. Even when all the relevant parameters are known, the most explicit formulations of the theory may be unable to specify, *unambiguously,* what constitutes rational behavior. This is a particularly vexing epistemological problem since explanations and predictions of rational-choice theories, like deterrence, reside either in reconstructing or forecasting an actor's decision-making calculus.

Rather than use a contrived example, I shall, in this chapter, demonstrate the above by examining the Berlin crisis of 1947 and showing why each of the two formal variants of deterrence

7

theory are deficient explanatory and predictive tools. Before proceeding, however, it will be useful to clarify, briefly, the limited sense in which I will use the term "rationality" throughout this essay.

1.1. On Rationality

With the exception of the concept of "power," of which more will be said below, there is perhaps no more "essentially contested concept" (MacIntyre 1973) in the strategic field than the concept of "rationality." In general, there are two main views of this concept. I will refer to the first as the *proceduralist* approach, and to the second as the *instrumentalist* approach.

In the proceduralists' view, rational behavior requires that an actor, after properly defining his goals (e.g., discovering the "national interest") and considering *all* possible alternatives, make "a cool and clearheaded means-ends calculation" (Verba 1961, 95) in which emotional, psychological, or more generally, nonlogical influences are ignored. Since such an actor is normally assumed to possess "infinite calculating ability" (Snyder and Diesing 1977, 341), he will select "from among alternative possible actions . . . that which, *from the point of view of an omniscient and objective observer, is most likely to promote the value pursued*" (Garnett 1975, 17).

Defined in this way, rational man is indeed an easily caricatured rara avis. As Hedley Bull (1961, 48) has noted, "a great deal of argument about military strategy . . . postulates 'rational action' of a kind of 'strategic man', a man who on further acquaintance reveals himself as a university professor of unusual intellectual subtlety."

Parody aside, to posit such exacting standards as prerequisites of rational behavior is to render the concept of rationality useless as an explanatory tool. When rationality is defined in terms of what are, essentially, unobservable cognitive processes,[1] it is almost impossible to operationalize, and hence, to distinguish from nonlogical or irrational behavior. Procedural definitions of rationality also tend to immerse analysts in endless, and irreconcilable, debates about the "rationality" of the goals that actors have chosen to pursue. Such an exercise does not advance the scientific enterprise of constructing explanatory or predictive models of behavior. For example, most people prefer life to death. But were the Jews at Masada, the Japanese kamikazes of World War II, or the Texans at the Alamo "irrational" because their preferences were inverted? Is it better to be red than dead, or the other way around? Each of us has an opinion on questions of this sort. But to brand those with contrary opinions as irrational serves little purpose.

Procedural definitions of rationality have, moreover, created an unfortunate and avoidable schism between theorists who, quite correctly, see behavior being influenced by the perceptions, and even the misperceptions, of fallible human actors and those who, in defining rationality instrumentally, start with the assumption that human activity is purposeful. As I will suggest below, there is no necessary contradiction between these two points of view.

In contrast to procedural definitions of rationality, instrumentalist definitions avoid judgments about the soundness of players' goals. Instead, rationality is defined as a *simple* ends-means calculation. A rational actor is one who makes a decision based upon goals as he or she defines them, and selects a strategy from among a set of options as he or she perceives them. Thus, subjective interpretations of the environment,

---

1. I do not mean to suggest that cognitive maps, belief systems, or operational codes cannot be reconstructed. What I have in mind here are fine distinctions between different forms of rationality based upon differences in mental processes decision-makers go through before formulating policy. For example, Snyder and Diesing (1977, chap. 5) attempt to distinguish between "maximizing" behavior and "satisficing" behavior by counting the number of alternatives consciously considered by the key actors in the crises in their data set.

personal idiosyncrasies, perceptual distortions due to stress, limited decision-time, surprise, or psychological predispositions do not stand in the way of a rational decision. Indeed, in the view of the instrumentalist, it is from this matrix of stimuli that a rational actor is assumed to decide (Rosenau 1967, 199; Stein 1982).

As defined by the instrumentalist, the rationality assumption is a useful and potent analytic device. Models based upon this conception of rationality can be used normatively to evaluate behavior against consistent and logically derived standards. (For an example of this usage, see chapter 6.) Such models can also be used descriptively to develop explanations of behavior by using the procedures of either *revealed* or *posited* preferences (Riker and Ordeshook 1973, 14). If one uses the former technique, as I do in chapter 7, the preferences of players can be deduced, or are revealed, from observations of their behavior. And if one uses the latter approach, as I do in chapter 5, explanations can be derived by demonstrating consistency between the posited preferences and actual decisions.[2]

Although powerful, the instrumentalist conception of rationality is not based on especially heroic assumptions. It does not require that actors be omniscient, omnipotent, or even have complete information.[3] Rather, in the instrumentalists' view, rationality requires only that players have *connected* and *transitive* preferences, that is, that they are able to evaluate and order outcomes in a logically consistent manner (Riker and Ordeshook 1973, 16–19).[4]

All of which is not to suggest, however, that the limited de-

2. For two other illustrations of this technique, see Zagare (1977, 1979).

3. The complete information assumption, however, is a particularly useful working assumption for constructing theories. Although this assumption will be used for this purpose in chapters 2, 3, and 4, it will be modified in the applications of chapters 5 and 6.

4. Since the model I develop in this work posits only dichotomous choices for the players, it does not require the assumption of a unitary decision-maker to avoid the problems associated with amalgamating individual preferences into a social choice (Arrow 1951). For an illuminating discussion of this issue, with relevant examples, see Bueno de Mesquita (1981).

scriptive ability of deterrence theory alluded to above is due to the (obviously misguided) application of the proceduralists' definition of rationality. In fact, even when the more modest definition of the instrumentalists is used, current manifestations of deterrence theory offer deficient explanations and predictions. I shall now demonstrate this by offering an exegesis of the resolution of the Berlin crisis of 1948 in terms of the two methodologies that have had the greatest impact upon the flavor and substance of the theory of deterrence, decision (expected utility) theory and one of its main branches, classical game theory.[5]

1.2 The Berlin Crisis of 1948

The origins of the 1948 Berlin crisis can be traced to a disagreement between the Western powers and the Soviet Union over the status of occupied Germany.[6] After World War II the Soviet Union, which wanted a string of weak buffer states around its western periphery, sought to keep Germany economically, politically, and militarily weak. By contrast, the Western powers, particularly the United States and Great Britain, desired to promote a strong, viable, pro-Western German state to act as a counterweight to Soviet expansion in Europe and to stand them in good stead as a trading partner.

The postwar administrative system for Germany made it difficult for the Western states to achieve their objectives. After Germany was defeated, it was divided into four zones, each

5. Of these two methodologies, George and Smoke (1974, 67) write: "Contemporary deterrence theory has been developed substantially as a deductivist product of the field known as 'decision theory.' Analysts have begun by applying the premises and logic of decision theory to the problem of deterrence and constructed abstract models which have then been presented as embracing the essential analytical issues. Often this use of decision theory has been in words, without recourse to symbols and other formalities of theory. But some discussions of deterrence have explicitly labeled their analyses 'decision theory' and have presented their conclusions in probabilistic form, . . . Often, however, probability has been left aside and the analysis has been cast in the forms of that branch of decision theory called 'game theory.'"

6. The following account of the Berlin crisis draws heavily from Davison (1958).

controlled by one of the four occupying powers, the United States, Great Britain, France, and the Soviet Union. Policy matters involving Germany as a whole were decided by the Allied Control Council, composed of the military commanders of each zone. Since this council operated under the principle of unanimity, each commander was able, in effect, to veto the decisions of this body. Thus, following World War II, the Soviets could, and did, block all Western attempts to revive Germany.

Continuing Western frustration stemming from the inability of the council to reach four-power agreement on the German question led to the convocation of the London Conference in February 1948. At this conference, representatives of the three Western powers, along with those of the Netherlands, Belgium, and Luxembourg, met to discuss a program to bring the non-Soviet sectors of Germany back into the mainstream of European political and economic life. An interim communiqué released at the beginning of March indicated that the participants at this conference were prepared to proceed with their plans with or without Soviet acquiescence.

The Soviets reacted with predictable displeasure to the communiqué. Contending that the conference was a violation of the Potsdam Agreement guaranteeing four-power control over Germany (which it was), the Soviets protested the announcement first by walking out of the Allied Control Council on March 20, and then by interfering with traffic between the Western-controlled zones of Germany and West Berlin.

The negative Soviet reaction, however, did not prevent the Western powers from going ahead with their plan. At the end of the conference in early June, an agreement was reached to coordinate policies in the American, British, and French zones, to include these zones in the European Recovery Program (the Marshall Plan), and to authorize the establishment of a German Federal Republic. Less than three weeks later, in the first step toward implementing these agreements, a currency reform was announced for West Germany (June 18) and West Berlin (June 19).

The currency reform was correctly interpreted by the Soviets as a Western attempt to circumvent the stalemate of the Allied Control Council and to exclude Soviet influence from West Germany. Rather than accede to a fait accompli, the Soviets resisted. On June 24, citing technical difficulties on the Berlin-Helmstead railroad line, they clamped a blockade around West Berlin and cut off electricity supplies to the city. By promising to lift the blockade, the Soviets hoped they could prevent the Western powers from pushing forward with their plan for creating a pro-Western German state out of their sectors. But even if the West did not agree to this trade, the Soviets calculated that, at a minimum, the blockade would enable them to gain control over all of Berlin.

The Western powers, in turn, interpreted the blockade as another in a series of expansionist Soviet moves in Eastern Europe. Collectively, the governments of the United States, Great Britain, and, albeit with some hesitation, France decided to meet the perceived Soviet threat and "contain" the Soviet aggression. Accordingly, an airlift of food and other supplies was launched to Berlin on June 26.

Initially, the airlift was thought to be a stopgap measure. Western leaders were pessimistic about their ability to supply Berlin with essential goods by air for an extended period of time. Much to their surprise, however, the airlift proved to be more effective than originally thought. Consequently, the Western powers were able to frustrate the Soviet maneuver.

At the time of the blockade, however, the strategic situation for the West appeared bleak. Since each side had essentially two broad strategies:[7] either to hold firm (H) or to back down (B), four outcomes of the crisis seemed possible:

A. *Continued Confrontation.* At the start of this crisis it appeared that if both superpowers held firm and the crisis continued, the Western powers would shortly lose control of West Berlin. The fall of the city, in turn,

---

7. The exact sense in which I use the term "strategy" will be explained in note 10.

would raise substantially the probability that the evolving cold war between the superpowers would escalate into a hot war.

B. *Soviet Victory*. If the Soviets held firm while the Western powers backed off and gave in to the Soviet stratagem in order to save West Berlin, the Western plan for a West German state would have to be dropped.

C. *Western Victory*. If the Western powers held firm and the Soviets were forced to back down and lift the blockade, a West German state would be established and Western access to Berlin maintained.

D. *The Status Quo Ante*. If both sides backed off, four-power control of Germany, as stipulated by the Potsdam Agreement, would be reestablished and perhaps a new spirit of superpower cooperation forged.[8]

What were the preferences of the two players over the set of outcomes? Surely, the Western powers and the Soviet Union each preferred to hold firm while the other backed off, thereby inducing a clear victory over the irresolute player (either outcome B or C). Failing this, each would have preferred a return to the status quo ante (outcome D) rather than accede to the victory of the other (either outcome B or C). And if, as Snyder and Diesing (1977, 113) assert, "both sides would probably have preferred giving up their goals to a serious outbreak of violence, risking a major war, then outcome A was their mutually worst outcome. Thus the Western preference order was (C,D,B,A) and the Soviet preference order (B,D,C,A).

In the more formal part of the strategic literature it is customary to use an *outcome matrix* to represent a deterrence relationship.[9] Following tradition, the strategies of the two players, the four possible outcomes, and the postulated preferences

8. For speculation to this effect, see Kennan (1967, 415–48).

9. As Freedman (1981, 182) points out, "for a time, until the mid-1960s, the employment of matrices was the *sine qua non* of a serious strategist."

	SOVIET UNION	
	Hold Firm	**Back Down**
WESTERN POWERS **Hold Firm**	A. SUPERPOWER CRISIS; control of West Berlin possibly lost by West; cold war intensifies. (1,1)	C. WESTERN VICTORY; German Federal Republic established; control of West Berlin retained by Western powers. (4,2)*
Back Down	B. SOVIET VICTORY; plans for a West German state dropped; West Berlin remains under Western control. (2,4)*	D. STATUS QUO ANTE; four-power control of Germany reestablished; West Berlin remains under Western control. (3,3)

Key: * = Nash equilibrium

FIGURE 1.1: Outcome Matrix of the 1947 Berlin Crisis

of the players over the set of outcomes are summarized in figure 1.1 in matrix form.[10] In this representation, the two strategies available to the Western powers have, arbitrarily, been

10. Throughout this essay, I shall refer to such figures as an *outcome,* or *payoff,*
matrix to distinguish them from what game theorists call the "normal-form." My reasons for maintaining this separation are twofold. First, it is almost impossible truly
to represent any nontrivial social situation in normal-form. (See, for example,
Rapoport's [1966, 41–43] attempt just to list the strategies available to the players in
the simple game of tic-tac-toe.) And second, and more importantly, a normal-form
representation suppresses several important elements of the "rules of the game," such
as the sequence of moves, the order of choice, and the nature of information available
to each player. (For a more detailed discussion of this point, see Zagare [1984a].) By
separating these concepts analytically, the implications for deterrence of both the nature of some elements of these rules and the underlying structural relationship of preferences and outcomes are highlighted. (Similar arguments to this effect can be found
in Hirshleifer [1985], who contends that a sharp distinction should always be maintained between the "payoff environment" and what he calls "the protocol of play;" in
Kilgour [1985], who, in reinterpreting the normal-form, develops the concept of an
"anticipation matrix"; and in Crawford [1985, 200], who argues that "many common

assigned to the rows of this matrix, while the two Soviet strategies have been assigned to the columns.[11]

In each cell of the matrix an ordered pair is used to depict the preference ranking of the two players over the set of outcomes. By convention, the first entry of each pair represents the ranking of the row player (here, the Western powers), and the second entry the ranking of the column player (here, the Soviet Union), respectively. In figure 1.1, the outcomes are ranked from highest to lowest, with "4" assigned to each player's best outcome, "3" to each player's next-best outcome, and so on. For example, the outcome (C) associated with the Western strategy of holding firm and Soviet back-down strategy (4,2), represents the best outcome for the Western powers and the next-worst outcome for the Soviet Union. The preferences of the players for the other three outcomes are interpreted in the same way.

The salient structural constraints that decision-makers on both sides labored under are neatly summarized in the payoff matrix of figure 1.1. It, therefore, provides the framework in which I will attempt to answer what are the two most important questions about this crisis. First, why did deterrence fail in Berlin in 1948, and second, given that it failed, why did the Western powers, not the Soviet Union, emerge victorious from this particular interaction? A final answer to these questions will not be given until chapter 4. For now, my purpose is only to demonstrate that, even ex post facto, current formulations of deterrence theory provide deficient answers to these questions.

---

confusions about how to analyze strategic interactions are eliminated by preserving a clear distinction between the structure of the game . . . and the theory of behavior being employed.")

In another break with convention, I will refer to a *strategy* as a choice that leads, however temporarily, to one of the outcomes listed in the payoff matrix. (In standard usage, a strategy is a complete contingency plan that specifies a particular choice for a player in every situation that might arise in a game.) And a switch from one strategy to another will be termed a *move*, which is normally taken to mean a decision point. As Brams (1983, 75) points out, standard usage of these terms could be maintained, but at the cost of much analytical complexity.

11. For a similar interpretation of this crisis, see Snyder and Diesing (1977, 113–14).

1.3 A Decision-Theoretic Explanation of the Berlin Crisis

As noted by George and Smoke (see footnote 5), much of extant theorizing about deterrence draws its inspiration from modern decision-theory. To understand the underlying conceptual similarities among those who use this approach to study deterrence, it will be useful to briefly consider a model of blackmail developed by Daniel Ellsberg (1959). Ellsberg's model, called the *critical risk model,* is not merely representative of this strand of theorizing. It has had an enormous impact, albeit indirectly through the work of Schelling (1960) and Snyder (1972), on both the substance and the spirit of deterrence theory.

In devising his model of blackmail, Ellsberg starts with three assumptions largely common to the deterrence literature:

1. *Incomplete information.* Each player is assumed to be unaware of both the strategy his opponent intends to use and the structure of his opponent's preferences over the set of outcomes.

2. *Cardinal utility.* The magnitudes of the payoffs in the outcome matrix are posited to reflect both the order and the intensity of each player's preferences, that is, each player's utility function is measured on an interval or cardinal scale.

3. *Probability estimates.* Each player is assumed to make *subjective* estimates, based on intelligence reports, past experiences, hunches, or the like, of the probability that an opponent will choose each of his available strategies.

Given these assumptions, what will motivate a player's choice of one strategy or another in a conflict situation? According to Ellsberg, a player will choose that strategy which maximizes his expected payoff. For example, if a player has two strategies, either to cooperate (C) or to defect (D) from cooperation, he will choose to cooperate when the expected payoff of cooperation, E(C), is greater than the expected payoff of defection, E(D). He will choose to defect when E(D) > E(C). Finally, a player's *critical risk* occurs when E(C) = E(D). At this point, any increase in a player's subjective estimate of the probability that his opponent will cooperate will make it rational for him to defect, and any increase in a player's estimate that his opponent will defect will make it rational for him to cooperate.

For an illustration of this calculation in the context of the Berlin crisis, assume that Western leaders estimated that the probability of continued Soviet intransigence throughout the crisis was "about one in four," which was, in fact, the estimate of the military commander of the American zone (General Lucius D. Clay) of the chance of war breaking out as the result of the crisis (Young 1968, 179). For purposes of illustration, also assume that the payoffs listed in figure 1.1 represent each player's cardinal evaluation of the four possible outcomes.[12] With these assumptions, the expected payoff of the West's two strategies can be determined by simply summing the product of the payoffs associated with each strategy and the probability that that outcome will occur. Thus, the expected payoff for the West of holding firm was:

$$E(H) = 1(.25) + 4(.75) = 3.25,$$

and the expected payoff for the West of backing down was:

$$E(B) = 2(.25) + 3(.75) = 2.75.$$

Since E(H) > E(B), the West obviously maximized its expected payoff by holding firm. Moreover, because the critical risk for the West was .50, holding firm would have maximized its expected payoff as long as the estimated probability of Soviet firmness was less than this figure. Were it higher than .50, the expected payoff for the Western powers would have been maximized by backing down. Thus, given the payoffs and

12. I make no representation that these values reflect the actual *cardinal* utilities of the two players during the Berlin crisis, although I believe that they represent a reasonable *ordinal* interpretation of their preferences. As explained in Zagare (1984), expected value calculations are appropriate only when each player's payoffs are measured on an interval scale. Hence, the subsequent computations only serve to illustrate the logic of Ellsberg's model.

probability estimates underlying these calculations, Ellsberg's critical-risk model seemingly provides a clear explanation of why the Western powers chose to resist the Soviet move in Berlin.

If players make strategy choices on the basis of expected value computations such as these, then a player can gain an advantage by manipulating those factors affecting them so that $E(C) > E(D)$ for one's opponent, that is, in a way that makes it rational for the other player to concede in a crisis or conflict-of-interest situation. This basic insight has led to the development of an influential subliterature of deterrence that Young (1975) calls "manipulative bargaining theory." [13] As its name suggests, the focus of this part of the deterrence literature is on devising or discovering tactics that can be used to rearrange the outcome matrix in an advantageous way.

Snyder (1972) divides these into "commitment tactics," which increase an opponent's estimate that a player will defect, and "critical risk tactics," which reduce an opponent's critical risk, thus making his cooperation more likely. Representative tactics include making "an irrevocable commitment" to a hard-line strategy, "burning one's bridges," feigning irrationality, and committing oneself in public to an unpopular or incredible position.

Both Western and Soviet behavior during the Berlin crisis supports Young's (1968, 337) hypothesis that "under conditions of crisis," one of these strategies, the "'initiative that forces an opponent to initiate' tends to become a critical coercive device." For example, as noted earlier, the Soviet blockade is generally interpreted to have been designed to present the West with the choice of either dropping its plan for a West German state or losing Berlin (George and Smoke 1974, 118). The blockade, ostensibly, left the next move up to the Western powers. The Western response to the blockade, in turn, was

---

13. According to Kaplan (1983), American tactics in Vietnam were heavily influenced by the ideas contained in Schelling (1960).

effective precisely because it enabled the Western powers to avoid this choice. The successful airlift, as much of a surprise to Western leaders as to the Soviets, allowed the Western powers to circumvent the Soviet initiative by choosing both not to forgo their plan to consolidate their zones of Germany and not to abandon Berlin. Moreover, this stratagem left the Soviets with the particularly unpalatable choice of risking a major war or backing down. The skillful use of this tactic, therefore, seems to account for the favorable resolution of the Berlin crisis for the Western powers. Parenthetically, this explanation is wholly consistent with the explanation implicit in Ellsberg's critical-risk model.

After reviewing this derivative literature, Young (1975, 314) concludes that this "conception of bargaining has a number of attractive features." It is difficult not to agree with this assessment. Perhaps the single most significant contribution of this approach is, as Morgenstern (1961, 105) once put it, that "it widens horizons and shows once more the immense complexity of the social world." Moreover, it forces a reexamination of the conventional wisdom that enjoins statesmen *not* to lose control of their emotions, *not* to negotiate with an opponent in public or in the press, and to remain flexible in their demands. If nothing else, the work of manipulative-bargaining theorists suggests that these popular maxims may be in need of reappraisal.

Still, in the words of one of the principal proponents of this methodology (Bueno de Mesquita, 1985a), the underlying expected utility paradigm suffers from a number of "serious" shortcomings that detract from the explanatory power of these models. First, because the expected utility approach suppresses important structural information about the relationship of player preferences, it ignores the impact that the interdependency of utilities can have on the rational choices that players make. As a result, a decision-theoretic analysis may overpredict conflict by specifying the necessary, but not the sufficient, conditions for interstate conflict and, in addition, is hard put to explain anomalous cases such as the occurrence of interventions or threats when the expected utility of two actors for conflict is lower than the expected utility of cooperation. In chapter 4, I will demonstrate that deterrence may constitute a stable relationship, i.e., is rational, even when two players have a higher expected utility for conflict. For now, however, I will show that conflict may be rational even when the expected utility of each player's conflictual strategy is less than the expected utility of the player's nonconflictual strategy.

To see this, consider again the payoff matrix of the Berlin crisis (fig. 1.1). In this game, conflict is the worst outcome for both the Western powers and the Soviet Union. Provided that the leaders on both sides attach some, even small, probability to the possibility that the other side will hold firm, it is not difficult to specify some hypothetical cardinal values to the (1,1) outcome so that $E(B) > E(H)$ for both players. If this outcome necessarily implied a general war, the cardinal values that would be attached to it would probably be very large negative numbers. Under these conditions, an expected utility analysis would predict that both sides would be deterred and back down.

Such a prediction would be deficient, however, because it would fail to take into account the strategic implications of the interdependency of these calculations. More specifically, even if the expected utility of holding firm for both players in this crisis were lower than that of their back-down strategy, the rational response of each would still be to hold firm, provided that the other player selected the strategy with the highest expected utility and decided to back down. Thus, it is possible that in the Berlin crisis each side had a higher expected utility for backing down, yet, precisely because of this interplay of expected utility scores, decided, at least initially, to hold firm.

But even this would be an unsatisfactory explanation for the behavior of both sides at the beginning of the Berlin crisis since the best counterresponse to the hold-firm strategy of the other would be to back off. And if both backed off, each player's best response would once again be to hold firm. And on it goes.

In some situations, then, expected utility models may be unable to produce determinate results, that is, specific statements about the relationship of expected utility scores and the eventual outcome selected by the players. Put in a slightly different way, because these models are unable to terminate the "he thinks, I think, he thinks" regress, they can provide, at best, the necessary but not the sufficient conditions for explaining interstate conflict or the absence thereof (Bueno de Mesquita 1981).[14] Thus, if expected utility models are interpreted as descriptive theory, they will be deficient because they cannot provide an explanation for deviant cases. And if interpreted as normative theory, the predictions of these models "would appear dangerous should they have an influence upon policy" (Morgenstern 1961, 105).

1.4 A Game-Theoretic Explanation of the Berlin Crisis

Unlike expected utility theory, game-theoretic models explicitly take into account the implications of strategic interdependence. In fact, it is probably this characteristic more than anything else that accounts for what Freedman (1981) calls the "brief flirtations" that some of the leading deterrence theorists have had with this paradigm. Nevertheless, in some cases, classical game-theoretic models, too, may fail to iden-

14. This is one reason why manipulative bargaining models are unable to specify the conditions under which various bargaining tactics are likely to be employed and the outcomes that result when they are (Young 1975, 316–17). For instance, this strand of theory cannot explain why the Western stratagem of airlifting supplies to Berlin eventually resulted in the Soviets backing down, while the analogous Soviet tactic that seemingly left the initiative up to the Western powers resulted in a firm Western response.

A more fundamental reason is that manipulative bargaining models ignore the psychology of threats and promises (Rapoport 1964). Because both of these critical-risk tactics may alter an opponent's preferences, their use may produce unintended results. Hitler's inferences about British concessions at Munich in 1938 constitute a case in point.

tify optimal behavior, and hence, lack explanatory and predictive power. To understand why, one must first come to appreciate the role that the concept of an *equilibrium outcome* (*point*) plays in "noncooperative" game theory.[15]

In noncooperative game theory, an outcome is said to be in equilibrium when no player in a game has an incentive, unilaterally, to upset it by switching to another strategy. Since equilibrium outcomes represent stable points in the set of possible societal states, they can be expected to be selected by rational agents on a regular basis. Explanations and predictions of game-theoretic models rest upon this premise. This is why game theorists hold that the identification of these regularly occurring outcomes in both the model world and the real world is a precondition to the discovery and specification of general laws of social behavior.

In classical game theory, the standard notion of stability is due to John Nash (1951). According to Nash, an outcome is an equilibrium if no single player in a game benefits *immediately* by switching to another strategy. For example, in the Berlin crisis game of figure 1.1, each outcome associated with a victory for one of the players is a *Nash equilibrium*. The (2,4) outcome, B, is stable since the Western powers would move from their next-worst outcome, 2, to their worst outcome, 1, should they switch from their back-down strategy associated with it to their hold-firm strategy, while the Soviets, by switching from their hold-firm strategy to their back-down strategy would move from their best outcome, 4, to their next-best outcome, 3. For similar reasons, outcome C (4,2) is also stable in

15. As distinct from *cooperative* game theory. In noncooperative game theory, players are assumed to be unable to make binding agreements with one another, while such agreements are assumed to be possible in the cooperative variant. Thus, in the noncooperative theory, the focus is on *internally* stable outcomes (i.e., equilibria) since it is assumed that there is no higher authority to enforce agreements. By contrast, the notion of an equilibrium (self-enforcing) outcome is of less relevance in cooperative game theory since binding agreements are assumed to be possible and outcomes can be stabilized *externally*. Because there is, at present, no overarching authority in the international system, it seems appropriate, in this book, to analyze the deterrence relationship from the vantage point of noncooperative game theory.

the sense of Nash. Thus, should the two players select strategies that lead to either of these outcomes, Nash's equilibrium concept suggests that it would emerge as the final outcome of the game.

By contrast, neither of the other two outcomes of the Berlin crisis is a Nash equilibrium. For instance, should both players decide to back down, outcome D, (3,3), would result. But at (3,3), each player has an immediate incentive, unilaterally, to change to another strategy. By switching to a hold-firm strategy, each player would move from a next-best outcome, 3, to a best outcome, 4. And since (1,1) is the worst outcome for both players, it clearly is not stable in the sense of Nash.

It has been known for some time that Nash's equilibrium concept suffers from a number of defects (Luce and Raiffa 1957, 105). To begin with, it is *static* since it implicitly assumes that players, in deciding whether or not to change strategies, make only an estimate of the immediate advantages and disadvantages of a unilateral move, and do not take into account the possible responses of other players. It is also *myopic* since it assumes that players do not (or can not) calculate the long-term consequences of moves and countermoves. Clearly, the underlying assumptions of Nash's equilibrium concept distort the dynamic nature of international politics, wherein strategy choices are usually made sequentially, and where probes and stratagems are frequently used—especially in deterrence or crisis situations (Young 1968, 218)—that permit responses to countermoves and counterprobes.

Putting these problems aside for the moment, we can see that Nash's equilibrium concept suffers from a more fundamental limitation that may render problematic explanations and predictions based upon it. When multiple Nash equilibria exist in a nonzero-sum game,[16] they may be neither *equivalent*, that

---

16. Nonzero-sum games are games in which players have both competitive and cooperative interests. For example, in the Berlin crisis game, both players are assumed to have a common interest in avoiding war. By contrast, in zero-sum games, the interests of the players are assumed to be diametrically opposed. Ever since Schelling's (1960) early work, deterrence has traditionally been analyzed as a nonzero-sum game.

is, have the same value, nor *interchangeable,* that is, found at the intersection of all equilibrium strategies.[17] This characteristic of Nash's equilibrium concept is significant because it means that, in some games, two or more equally attractive equilibrium outcomes may exist, each possessing equivalent status as a solution, with no compelling reason to choose among them, and no guarantee that nonequilibria will not result when players choose strategies associated with an equilibrium outcome.

It is easy to show that the two Nash equilibria in the Berlin crisis game are neither equivalent nor interchangeable. They are not equivalent because they yield different payoffs to each player. And they are not interchangeable since all equilibrium strategy pairs do not lead to an equilibrium outcome. For instance, were each player to select the strategy associated with the equilibrium each prefers most (i.e., hold firm), the outcome would be (1,1), which is not a Nash equilibrium.

The possible existence of two or more nonequivalent or noninterchangeable Nash equilibria presents a potential stumbling block for the development of a positive theory of deterrence within a noncooperative game-theoretic framework, namely, the problem of justifying the selection of one outcome or another as the final outcome of the game. Unless competing equilibria can be eliminated in situations in which multiple equilibria are found,[18] explanations and predictions derived from game-theoretic models will be weak and less than satisfying. For example, the fact that there are two Nash equilibria in the Berlin crisis game sheds very little light on one of the key questions about it: Why did the Western powers, and not the Soviet Union, prevail in this particular crisis? Consequently, unless sound theoretical reasons can be found for distinguishing between equilibria in games like this one, very little can be

17. A related problem stems from the fact that in some games, (pure) strategy equilibria may not exist. For a discussion of the qualification, see Zagare (1984, chap. 2).

18. Or unless specific equilibria can be discovered where none ostensibly exist.

said about how or why some conflicts are resolved, and very
little insight is gained into the nature of some conflict interactions. It is partly for this reason that Ordeshook (1980, 450)
argues that "the scientific task before us . . . appears no different from the one von Neumann and Morgenstern confronted: generalizing and redefining the meaning of the word
'equilibrium'."

The traditional response of game theorists to the indetermi-
nancy problems associated with nonzero-sum games has been
either to augment the concept of a rational decision by making
stronger assumptions or to incorporate additional environmental detail into more content-specific models. The supposition
beneath both of these research strategies is that the indeter-
minancy problem may be eliminated by departing from the
rarefied atmosphere of game-theoretic models partially devoid
of real-world context (Riker and Ordeshook 1973).

Although a number of theoretical refinements have been developed in recent years by researchers using these techniques,[19]
none of these provide a firm foundation for constructing a general theory of deterrence. For instance, Nigel Howard's (1971)
extension of classical game theory, called the theory of metagames, is deficient because it does not alleviate the indeterminacy problem associated with the Berlin crisis and similar
games. In fact, since three of the four outcomes emerge as
"metaequilibria" in this particular game, the problem is actually compounded.[20] The same is also true of the "improved
metagame" technique recently developed by Fraser and Hipel
(1979).[21]

Similarly, a number of interrelated models of deterrence and
the escalation/deescalation process advanced by Brams and
Kilgour (1985a, 1985b, 1985c) suffer from the inconsistent

19. For a recent review of these developments in political science, see Zagare
(1986); in economics, Schotter and Schwödiauer (1980); in psychology, Colman
(1982); and more generally, Shubik (1982).

20. A detailed discussion of the theory of metagames in terms of a game with the
same structure as the Berlin crisis game can be found in Brams (1976).

21. For a discussion and relevant citations, see Zagare (1986).

application of the rationality postulate (Achen 1986). In the models that they construct, each player's decision to attack or not to attack is based upon the assumption that his opponent is simultaneously rational and irrational, albeit irrational with some probability. More specifically, in modeling deterrence as a game of Chicken, Brams and Kilgour assume that each player, in being deterred, will respond rationally to some variable probability of retaliation, and that each player, in deterring his opponent, will respond irrationally with some probability in carrying out a threat that he would prefer not to execute. Thus, while Brams and Kilgour demonstrate that a player might have an incentive in some deterrence games to precommit himself to carry out an irrational threat, they do not provide an explanation of why a player's opponent would find such a precommitment credible. It is for this reason that the implications of this research for understanding the dynamics of deterrence relationships is unclear.

Finally, Robert Axelrod's (1984) exploration of the conditions under which individuals and small, homogeneous groups can do better by cooperating, when members of a larger group are noncooperative, is only tangentially related to the problems unique to deterrence. Axelrod's model, which envisions a large number of players interacting with one another, is based upon the premise that these interactions are randomly distributed. Most deterrence games, however, involve nonrandom associations with a small number of predictable and recognizable opponents.[22]

---

22. Interestingly, however, there are a number of similarities between both Axelrod's model and the model that I develop in this book. For instance, Axelrod investigates the problems associated with the evolution of cooperative behavior in the context of an iterated Prisoners' Dilemma game and demonstrates that cooperation can emerge in a world of unconditional noncooperation if, inter alia, the cooperating players all use a *maximally discriminating* strategy like tit-for-tat. He also shows that a group of cooperating individuals may, under certain conditions, be able to resist invasion by unconditionally noncooperative players called *meanies*. Similarly, in the next chapter I shall argue that in mutual deterrence situations that share the structural characteristics of this particular game, tit-for-tat strategies are necessary for deterrence stability.

2
The Logic of
Mutual Deterrence

In the social sciences, the theory of mutual deterrence stands on hallowed ground. When it is considered as a prescriptive theory, or policy, it is frequently credited with preserving the stability of the international system since the end of the Second World War; and when it is considered as a descriptive theory, it is often revered as the only extant, fully developed, positive theory in international relations.[1]

As suggested in the last chapter, however, the theory of deterrence rests upon a rather shaky foundation. In this chapter and the next two, therefore, I will attempt to reformulate the theory of deterrence and place it on firmer theoretical footing. I begin this reconstruction by first discussing the structural characteristics of the relationship of mutual deterrence in its prototypical form and showing that a formalization of these conditions leads to an apparent inconsistency between the theory of deterrence and the conventional wisdom of classical game theory. More specifically, I demonstrate that propositions implicit in the theory of mutual deterrence suggest a basic congruence between the structure of the ideal deterrence relationship and the game of Prisoners' Dilemma, a pathological game generally thought of as a corruption of rational choice. I next show how this anomaly can be resolved within an alternate game-theoretic framework called the *theory of*

1. This chapter draws on material contained in Frank C. Zagare, "Toward a Reformulation of the Theory of Mutual Deterrence," *International Studies Quarterly* 29 (June 1985), and "Limited-Move Equilibria in 2 × 2 Games," *Theory and Decision* 16 (January 1984).

moves. Following this, I extend the model by developing the methodology needed to take into account the impact of some relevant empirical constraints on deterrence stability. Finally, I further explore the mutual deterrence relationship by examining the dynamics of those games that fall short of ideal conditions.

2.1 The Structural Characteristics of Mutual Deterrence Games

Implicit in the fact that each of two players is attempting to deter the other are several assumptions about the utility functions, (u), of the players over the set of possible outcomes of a typical deterrence game. Still other assumptions are implied by the nature of each player's retaliatory threat. In this section, I will investigate the structural implications that these assumptions have for the relationship of mutual deterrence in its ideal form, that is, when both players have a credible and capable threat.

To this end, consider for now the generalized representation of a deterrence game depicted in figure 2.1. In this representation, each of two players, A and B, are assumed to have two

PLAYER B

		b_1	b_2
		STATUS QUO	VICTORY FOR B
	a_1	(a_1, b_1)	(a_1, b_2)
PLAYER A			
	a_2	VICTORY FOR A	MUTUAL LOSS
		(a_2, b_1)	(a_2, b_2)

FIGURE 2.1: Generalized Representation of a 2 × 2 Deterrence Game

strategies, one that supports the status quo (either a_1 or b_1), and one that does not (either a_2 or b_2). These two strategies, in turn, give rise to $2 \times 2 = 4$ possible outcomes which are summarized verbally in figure 2.1. As before, these outcomes are represented by an ordered pair in each cell of the outcome matrix with the first entry of each pair denoting the payoff of the row player, (A), and the second entry the payoff of the column player, (B), should that outcome be selected by the players. For example, if both players choose their first strategy, the outcome associated with the status quo, (a_1, b_1), results. In this case, the utility that A associates with this outcome, $u_A(a_1, b_1)$, is given by a_1, while the utility that B associates with this same outcome, $u_B(a_1, b_1)$, is given by b_1.

In a descriptive sense, the payoff matrix of figure 2.1 is a simplification of most actual deterrence situations, especially of those that evolve out of intense crises. In the real world, a number of qualitatively different strategies typically exist for each player, ranging from weak to strong support of the status quo on the one hand, to minor to major deviations from it on the other. And an analogous increase in the number of distinct outcomes is implied when an expanded list of strategies is considered. For instance, depending upon the actual strategies selected by the players, a whole set of mutual punishment outcomes, varying in intensity from slight to severe, and in nature from symmetric to asymmetric, could conceivably be identified.

In spite of the above, there is a good reason for focusing on the seminal form depicted in figure 2.1. The salient structural characteristics of deterrence situations in general seem to be captured with a simple 2×2 payoff matrix (Snyder and Diesing 1977, 83). A more complex and, perhaps, descriptively richer representation would obscure, rather than highlight, these fundamental relationships. Since most formal treatments of deterrence have concentrated on 2×2 games, there seems to be a consensus in the literature on this point. Thus, as a first approximation, it does not seem unwarranted to direct attention to the limiting case.[2]

The Status Quo

The theory of deterrence starts with the assumption that a status-quo outcome exists from which the departure of the other player is undesirable from the vantage point of his opponent. Without loss of generality, then, designate (a_1,b_1) the status-quo outcome. Since it is assumed that both players prefer the status quo to the outcome that results when the *other* player departs from it, i.e., when A moves to (a_2,b_1) or when B moves to (a_1,b_2), it can be inferred that the theory of deterrence is directed at situations where:

$$\text{for A, } u_A (a_1,b_1) > u_A (a_1,b_2), \text{ and} \qquad [2.1a]$$
$$\text{for B, } u_B (a_1,b_1) > u_B (a_2,b_1). \qquad [2.1b]$$

Put differently, equation [2.1a] says that Player A prefers the outcome associated with the status quo, (a_1,b_1), to the outcome associated with a victory for B, (a_1,b_2). Equation [2.1b] is similarly interpreted.

While the requirements expressed in equation [2.1] are necessary for a game to qualify as a deterrence game, they clearly are not sufficient. For the notion of deterrence to be relevant, at least one player must have an incentive to move away from the status quo. Games wherein this minimal condition is satisfied will be termed *unilateral deterrence* games. When both players have an incentive to upset the status quo, a game of *mutual deterrence* will be said to exist.[3]

2. This is not to suggest, though, that more complicated game forms, that recognize finer distinctions among both strategies and outcomes, are unimportant or that they should be disregarded. Indeed, it is my intention, ultimately, to fully extend the approach advanced herein so that these more complex structures can be explored within a single, logically consistent, and intuitively satisfying conceptual framework.

3. This is a departure from conventional usage. These terms are normally used to indicate a deterrence relationship wherein either one player has a nuclear capability (unilateral deterrence) or both players have one (mutual deterrence). For a discussion, see Morgan (1983).

Since a relationship of mutual deterrence specifically envisions a situation where *both* players would benefit by upsetting the status quo, it follows that in such a game the following restrictions on the preference orders of the two players will also hold:

for A, $u_A (a_2,b_1) > u_A (a_1,b_1)$, and   [2.2a]

for B, $u_B (a_1,b_2) > u_B (a_1,b_1)$.   [2.2b]

Putting [2.1] and [2.2] together produces:

for A, $u_A(a_2,b_1) > u_A (a_1,b_1) > u_A (a_1,b_2)$, and   [2.3a]

for B, $u_B(a_1,b_2) > u_B (a_1,b_1) > u_B (a_2,b_1)$.   [2.3b]

In words, this ranking implies that, ceteris paribus, each player would prefer to upset the status quo unilaterally, and would prefer that the other player not upset it. Thus, the restrictions implied by equation [2.3] are completely consistent with the verbal descriptions of three of the four outcomes given in figure 2.1: each player prefers to win the game, but prefers the status quo to the outcome associated with a victory for his opponent. By definition, then, the preference rankings expressed in equation [2.3] constitute the delimiting structural characteristics of the relationship of mutual deterrence.

The Nature of the Threat

The idea that two players in a game are both trying to prevent the other from overturning the status quo implies a rather obvious relationship among three of the four outcomes in the deterrence game—see equation [2.3]—for each player. But to complete the (ordinal) ranking of the outcomes, and hence, to fully determine the nature of the deterrence game, it is necessary to specify the preference relationship of these three outcomes to (a_2,b_2).

Outcome (a_2,b_2) represents the outcome that would be induced if one player upset the status quo in order to gain a unilateral advantage and the other player resisted and attempted to punish the first and deny his opponent these advantages. Put differently, (a_2,b_2) represents the threat upon which the deterrence relationship rests.

Patently, each player's evaluation of this threat outcome is a function of the *capability* of the other; and each player's perception of the other's evaluation of this outcome depends upon the *credibility* of the other player's threat. Thus, if capability is defined as the ability to hurt (Schelling 1966), each player will have a capable threat if and only if the other player prefers that, if he takes the prohibited action, the threat not be carried out. It follows, therefore, that if both players possess a capable threat:

$$\text{for A, } u_A(a_2,b_1) > u_A(a_2,b_2), \text{ and} \qquad [2.4a]$$
$$\text{for B, } u_B(a_1,b_2) > u_B(a_2,b_2). \qquad [2.4b]$$

But surely this is a minimum condition for a capable threat. Clausewitz is not the only analyst who has noted that an aggressor will always prefer to achieve his ends peacefully rather than pay the price for a transgression. A capable threat must also be measured against the value of the status quo. A player is hurt by an executed threat not only when his opponent resists, but also when the gains he may ultimately secure are less than the value he attaches to his present situation. In other words, net gains or losses are properly gauged against some initial position. Thus, a second, and more stringent, requirement for a capable threat is that this initial payoff exceed the payoff a player receives if the threat is executed. If both players have a capable threat, then, the following restrictions will also be assumed to apply:

$$\text{for A, } u_A(a_1,b_1) > u_A(a_2,b_2), \text{ and} \qquad [2.5a]$$
$$\text{for B, } u_B(a_1,b_1) > u_B(a_2,b_2). \qquad [2.5b]$$

By contrast, if one player has a capable threat and the other does not, the preference ranking of the opponent of the player whose threat is capable would simply reverse the restriction of equation [2.5]. And if neither player is capable of hurting the other, the preferences of both players would be reversed.

Finally, credibility. By most accounts, credibility is the "magic ingredient" of every deterrence relationship (Freedman

1981, 96). Credibility means that the player being deterred must believe that the threat *will* be carried out if he takes the prohibited action. The question of how threats can be made credible is an interesting one that has received considerable attention in the literature of deterrence, but regardless of the tactics used to ensure that the threat is seen as credible, a minimum condition that must be satisfied by a credible threat is that the threatened player must believe that the other player prefers the outcome associated with the execution of the threat, (a_2, b_2), to the outcome associated with the threatened player's unilateral departure from the status quo (Fraser and Hipel 1979, 802).[4] The essence of credibility, therefore, resides in a subjective evaluation on the part of the player being deterred of the willingness, or preference, of the other player to execute his threat. Unless the player being deterred perceives that the other prefers to resist, rather than accept, a unilateral departure from the status quo, a threat will not be seen to be credible.

Note that the notion of credibility rests upon the interpretation of one player's preferences by the other and, hence, bears no necessary correspondence with objective reality. A player may fully intend (i.e., prefer) to carry out a retaliatory threat, but unless the other player believes this to be so, the threat is not credible. Conversely, a player may threaten retaliation but have no intention at all of executing the threat. Still, if the threat is not seen as a bluff, it will be credible.

Whatever the case, however, if both players in a game of mutual deterrence have an (inherently) credible threat,[5] the following restrictions will hold:

---

4. This seems especially true of deterrence in one-shot games, of which strategic nuclear deterrence is perhaps the best example. In repeated play situations, one could plausibly make the argument that the credibility of a threat derives from payoffs in subsequent games and that condition [2.6] is not necessary. (For this argument, see Brams and Hessel [1984].) In my opinion, however, this argument is just another way of saying that each player prefers (a_2, b_2)—whatever its short-term implications are—to the outcome associated with a victory by his opponent—either (a_2, b_1) or (a_1, b_2).)

5. The reason for the qualification will be given in chapter 4.

B perceives that for A, $u_A (a_2,b_2) > u_A (a_1,b_2)$, [2.6a]
and

A perceives that for B, $u_B (a_2,b_2) > u_B (a_2,b_1)$. [2.6b]
As before, the lack of a credible threat by one or both players
can be reflected by appropriate modifications of the direction
of the inequalities in these equations.

Depending upon the nature of each player's threat, a number
of structurally distinct games of mutual deterrence—each satisfying the minimal restrictions of equation [2.3]—can be
identified. For example, if both players in a mutual deterrence
game are assumed to have a credible and a capable threat—
two conditions that deterrence theorists argue are necessary
for the stability of this relationship (Kaufmann 1956)—then
the structural characteristics of the resulting game can be generated simply by combining the requirements of equation [2.3]
with those of equations [2.4], [2.5], and [2.6]. This particular
combination produces the following restrictions on the preference orders of the two players:

for A, $u_A(a_2,b_1) > u_A(a_1,b_1) > u_A(a_2,b_2) > u_A(a_1,b_2)$, [2.7a]
and

for B, $u_B(a_1,b_2) > u_B(a_1,b_1) > u_B(a_2,b_2) > u_B(a_2,b_1)$. [2.7b]
If a rank of "4" is assigned to each player's best outcome, "3"
to his next best outcome, and so on, the ranking of the outcomes expressed in [2.7] gives rise to the payoff matrix depicted in figure 2.2, which defines the well-known game of
"Prisoners' Dilemma."

2.2 The Paradox of Mutual Deterrence

In the previous section, it was demonstrated that arguments
implicit in the theory of mutual deterrence suggest that the
archetypical relationship among the outcomes for players in a
deterrence game is that of Prisoners' Dilemma.[6] This connec-

---

6. For a similar conclusion, see Kavka (1982, 102) and Wagner (1983).

PLAYER B

		b_1	b_2
		STATUS QUO	VICTORY FOR B
	a_1	(3,3)*	(1,4)
PLAYER A			
		VICTORY FOR A	MUTUAL LOSS
	a_2	(4,1)	(2,2)*

Key: * = nonmyopic equilibrium

FIGURE 2.2: The Mutual Deterrence Game (Prisoners' Dilemma)

tion between game theory's most famous game and the theory of mutual deterrence is very surprising. Typically, it is the game of Chicken, not Prisoners' Dilemma, that is discussed by theorists in conjunction with the problems associated with mutual deterrence and the balance of terror (see, inter alia, Jervis 1979, 291; Rapoport 1964, 116; Hopkins and Mansbach 1973, 368–69; Brams 1975, 1985; Schelling 1960, 1966).

This raises an interesting question: why have deterrence theorists almost uniformly gravitated toward the Chicken analogy when their verbal descriptions of the conditions necessary for stable mutual deterrence, i.e., a credible and capable threat, so obviously imply the structure of a Prisoners' Dilemma game? One can only guess at the answer to this question. There are, perhaps, three possibilities.

The first is that the Chicken analogy is consistent with the popular conception that in the nuclear age the outcome that results when two states carry out their deterrent threat, i.e., (a_2,b_2), is the worst of all possible outcomes for both players (see fig. 2.4). A related explanation is that the Chicken analogy is used so frequently because it represents a worst-case scenario that highlights the particular problems addressed by the theory of deterrence.

While one or both of these explanations may account for the initial attraction of deterrence theorists to Chicken, neither one can explain why the structural solution to the problem implied in their analyses (i.e., somehow transforming the game from Chicken to Prisoners' Dilemma) has never been acknowledged or made explicit. The third explanation does explain why, and hence seems the most compelling.

As already indicated, Prisoners' Dilemma is generally regarded as a pathological game and is frequently used as a model of degenerative political processes such as the non-acquisition of a public good (Hardin 1971), preemptive military strikes (Hopkins and Mansbach 1973, chap. 17), nuclear proliferation (Bueno de Mesquita and Riker 1982) and arms races (Baugh 1984). The reason for the notorious reputation of the Prisoners' Dilemma game is simple: both players in this game have a *strictly dominant* strategy[7] that leads to a unique, *Pareto-inferior*[8] Nash equilibrium outcome, (2,2).[9] Thus, for deterrence theorists to offer the structure of this game as the solution to the problem of mutual deterrence, and to suggest the status quo, (3,3), as the outcome that should be chosen by rational players, they would have had to confront the conventional wisdom of game theory and find a convincing counter-argument to the dominance principle. By contrast, it was easier to develop models suggesting that rational players should choose their strategy associated with (3,3) in Chicken. Even though (3,3) is not stable in either game in the sense of being a

7. A strictly dominant strategy produces an outcome that is better than the outcome produced by any other strategy, regardless of the strategy selected by the other player.

8. An outcome is said to be Pareto-inferior (or Pareto-deficient) if another outcome in a game exists that is better for one player and no worse for the other. Since in Prisoners' Dilemma both players prefer (3,3) to (2,2), the latter outcome is Pareto-inferior. Conversely, the three other outcomes are all Pareto-optimal, that is, each is preferred to any other outcome by *at least* one player. For instance, (3,3) is preferred to (1,4) by Player A, to (4,1) by Player B, and to (2,2) by both players. Among the 78 distinct 2 × 2 games identified by Rapoport and Guyer (1976), Prisoners' Dilemma alone is uniquely characterized by these two features, i.e., dominant strategies leading to a Pareto-deficient Nash equilibrium.

9. For a more detailed discussion of this game, and of attempts to overcome this dilemma, see Zagare (1984a) and the literature cited therein.

Nash equilibrium, a strategy supporting this outcome is at least a *minimax* strategy in Chicken.[10]

Whatever the explanation for the popularity of the Chicken analogy, however, it is clear that it is incomplete and misleading, and that this analogy tells only part of the story. Chicken may very well encapsulate the *problem* of mutual deterrence, especially in the nuclear age, wherein threats are inherently incredible. But if, as the theory of deterrence suggests, stable mutual deterrence requires that both players possess a credible threat, then Prisoners' Dilemma exemplifies its *solution*.

2.3 A Reconciliation of Game Theory and the Theory of Mutual Deterrence

Is the theory of mutual deterrence fatally flawed by the posited connection between the archetypical situation of mutual deterrence and the structure of Prisoners' Dilemma? In this section, I will argue that it is not, that the theory of mutual deterrence can be reconciled with the conventional wisdom of game theory by incorporating into a formal game-theoretic framework the assumptions implicitly specified by deterrence theorists about the rules governing the strategy choices of the players. I will also argue that the particular assumptions made by deterrence theorists about these rules explain both the dissatisfaction of some of them with classical game-theoretic models and the essential nature of the modified expected-utility models developed by manipulative bargaining theorists to deal with the dynamics of deterrence. Finally, I will show that many of the inadequacies of these models can be overcome by embedding the deterrence relationship in a dynamic game-theoretic framework called the *theory of moves*.

---

10. The concept of a minimax (or maximin) strategy, which is the cornerstone of the theory of zero-sum games, rests upon the conservative principle that a player should attempt to *mini*mize his *max*imum possible loss in a game. For a further discussion of this concept, see Zagare (1984a). And for an example of the argument that this principle justifies the selection of the strategies associated with the (3,3) outcome in Chicken, see Deutsch (1978, 143–45).

To develop these points, it will be useful to consider the very different assumptions made by deterrence theorists and game theorists about the circumstances under which strategy choices are made. For their part, game theorists typically begin with the assumption that strategy choices are made simultaneously (or, equivalently, in ignorance of the choice of the other player) and unconditionally. Such an assumption, of course, naturally leads them to the conclusion that in a one-shot Prisoners' Dilemma game, each player should choose his dominant strategy. Herein lies the essence of the dilemma, since the dominant strategies of the players are associated with a Pareto-inferior Nash equilibrium.

By contrast, in their analyses deterrence theorists almost uniformly envision a world in which strategy choices are made both sequentially and conditionally. Or as George and Smoke (1974, 48) put it, "deterrence is merely a contingent threat: 'If you do x I shall do y to you.'"

These different assumptions about the rules governing strategy choices made it necessary for "second wave" deterrence theorists to develop models that were more compatible with the type of decision they had in mind. In so doing, it should not be surprising that these theorists did not rush to embrace the concept of a Nash equilibrium—the basis of most non-cooperative solution concepts in game theory. As previously indicated, Nash defined an outcome to be in equilibrium if neither player in a game could benefit immediately by departing unilaterally from it. In Nash's conception of an equilibrium outcome, then, the relevant comparison for a player contemplating a strategy switch is between the status quo (a_1,b_1) and the outcome he could induce by changing his strategy, i.e., either (a_2,b_1) or (a_1,b_2). But in a deterrence situation, the relevant comparison is between the status quo and the outcome associated with the deterrent threat, i.e., (a_2,b_2).[11] Conse-

_____

11. This is why the fact that (3,3) is not a Nash equilibrium in Chicken is of little moment for deterrence theorists.

quently, Nash's equilibrium concept was not seen as an adequate basis upon which to construct a theory of deterrence.[12]

On the other hand, many of the other simplifying assumptions employed by game theorists are compatible with the calculus of deterrence.[13] Moreover, deterrence theorists were naturally attracted to the parsimonious manner in which game theorists depicted the structure of an interactive decision. Consequently, the new models developed by some of the most influential deterrence theorists reflected this duality: although much of the outward appearance of game theory was retained (e.g., matrix-form representation), the underlying logic of the game theorist, based on simultaneous and unconditional strategy choices and the concept of a Nash equilibrium, was abandoned.[14] In its place, many deterrence theorists substituted a looser logic based upon manipulation of the outcome matrix, variable payoffs, and expected utility calculations.

As was seen in chapter 1, however, this approach is not without its own limitations. The models developed by the manipulative bargaining theorists have been criticized because they fail to produce determinate outcomes, are unable to terminate the "he thinks, I think, he thinks" regress and, since they are based upon the idea of cardinal utility, are difficult to test outside of some highly structured experimental settings. These difficulties, in turn, reflect unfavorably on the theory of deterrence.

Deterrence theory, however, can be rescued from these inadequacies and, at the same time, stated in a logically consistent and parsimonious way, when viewed through the lenses of an alternate game-theoretic framework called the *theory of*

12. Much the same could be said about the zero-sum assumption that was also characteristic of much of the early game-theoretic literature. For an explicit statement to this effect, see Schelling (1960).

13. For a discussion of some of these assumptions, see George and Smoke (1974, 71–82).

14. Snyder and Diesing's (1977) premature and unfounded rejection of game-theoretic models is representative of the ambivalent attitude of deterrence theorists toward game theory's formal logic.

moves. As developed by Brams and Wittman (1981) and extended by others, "the theory of moves describes optimal strategic calculations in normal-form games in which the players can move and countermove from an initial outcome in sequential play" (Brams 1983).

At the heart of the theory of moves is the concept of a *nonmyopic equilibrium* (Brams and Wittman 1981). Unlike Nash's notion of an equilibrium outcome, the concept of a nonmyopic equilibrium assumes that each player in a sequential game can make conditional *and* sequential moves from an initial outcome or status-quo point,[15] and is able to evaluate the long-term consequences of such a departure. More specifically, the concept of a nonmyopic equilibrium assumes that the following rules of play operate in a 2 × 2 ordinal game:

1. Both players simultaneously choose strategies, thereby defining an *initial outcome* of the game or, alternately, in the interpretation used in this essay, an initial outcome (or status quo) is imposed on the players by empirical circumstances.

2. Once at an initial outcome, either player can unilaterally switch his strategy and change the outcome to a subsequent outcome.

3. The other player can respond by unilaterally switching his strategy, thereby changing the subsequent outcome to a new subsequent outcome.

4. These strictly alternating moves continue until the player with the next move chooses not to switch his strategy. When this happens, the game terminates, and the out-

15. The theory of metagames, developed by Howard (1971), attempts to retain Nash's equilibrium concept under these conditions. For a discussion of some of the problems this raises, see Brams (1976, chap. 4) and the literature cited therein. And for a brief review of other attempts to develop dynamic game models, see Brams and Wittman (1981).

come reached is the *final outcome* (Brams and Hessel 1982).[16]

These rules bear more than a passing resemblance to the conditions typically present in deterrence games. As Wagner (1982, 342) has recently noted, "a feature common to all situations involving the use of military force is that one government does something, whereupon another either does or does not reply to the second's response, and so forth." Thus, the dynamic-choice framework associated with the theory of moves renders it an extremely attractive methodology for assessing the conditions associated with deterrence stability, or the lack thereof.

Given these rules, and the ability of the players to calculate the consequences of a departure from an initial outcome, two conditions must be met for an initial outcome to be considered a nonmyopic equilibrium: First, neither player must perceive an advantage in departing from it, and second, there must be *termination* of the move-countermove sequence, that is, the sequence of moves and countermoves must not cycle back to the initial outcome. Brams and Wittman assume that there will be termination if an outcome is reached in the sequential move process whereby the player with the next move can ensure his best outcome by staying at it.[17]

The concept of a nonmyopic equilibrium, then, is a look-ahead idea that assumes that a player will evaluate the long-term consequences of departing from an initial outcome, taking into account the probable response of the other player, his own counterresponse, subsequent counterresponses, and so on. If for *both* players the starting outcome is preferred to

16. As *initial* assumptions, these rules provide a useful starting point for analysis. Moreover, as will be demonstrated shortly, they can easily be modified to conform to the reality of a wide range of actual deterrence situations.

17. For a related termination condition, called *rational termination,* that defines a player's "staying power," see Brams and Hessel (1983). And for a more general specification of this equilibrium concept, in which the termination condition is dropped, see Kilgour (1984, 1985).

the outcome each player calculates he will end up at by making an initial departure, the starting outcome is a nonmyopic equilibrium.

It is easy to show that the status-quo outcome in the mutual deterrence (Prisoners' Dilemma) game of figure 2.2 satisfies both of these requirements. This is significant because it suggests that in its prototypical form, when both players have a credible and capable threat, mutual deterrence constitutes a stable relationship. Moreover, the fact that the status quo is stable in the nonmyopic sense resolves the apparent contradiction between the prescriptions of the deterrence theorist and those of the game theorist.

To see this, consider now the game tree depicted in figure 2.3, which lists the sequence of moves and countermoves implied by a departure by Player A away from the status-quo outcome, (3,3), in the Prisoners' Dilemma game of figure 2.2. Player A's incentive to move from this outcome can be determined simply by working backwards up the game tree and asking what the rational choice of each player is at each node or decision point. If the outcome that is implied by this process is inferior to (3,3) for the player postulated to have the first move—in this case, Player A—then this outcome is stable in the nonmyopic sense for this player. If a similar calculation also reveals that this outcome is stable in the nonmyopic sense for Player B, then it is a nonmyopic equilibrium. On the other hand, if the outcome implied by a departure from an initial outcome by either player when he is postulated to have the first move on the tree is superior to the initial outcome, then this outcome is not stable in the nonmyopic or long-term sense.

At the last node on the tree of figure 2.3, Player B must choose between staying at (1,4)—his best outcome—or moving to (3,3)—his next-best outcome. Clearly, should this node be reached in a sequence of moves and countermoves, Player B will choose not to move to (3,3)—indicated by a slash through the branch leading to this outcome—but rather would choose to stay at (1,4).

But would such a sequence ever rationally get to this point if (3,3) is the initial outcome? To determine this, consider Player A's choice at the previous node, (2,2). At this node, Player A is faced with a choice of staying at (2,2)—his next-worst outcome—or moving to (1,4)—his worst outcome. Given this choice, A would not switch strategies, thereby terminating the sequence of moves and countermoves before Player B can choose at (1,4).

Given Player A's rational choice at (2,2), what should Player B do at the preceding node? Here Player B can decide to stay at (4,1)—his worst outcome—or move to (2,2)—his next-worst outcome—which, because of the expected choice of Player A, would become the final outcome. For Player B, then, the rational choice is to move to (2,2).

What should Player A do at the first node, (3,3)? Player A can either stay at (3,3)—his next-best outcome—or move to his best outcome at (4,1). However, as was just illustrated, a move to (4,1) implies (2,2) as the final outcome in a sequence of moves and countermoves. Since Player A prefers (3,3) to (2,2), he should rationally choose to stay at the original status quo. And since Player A has no long-term incentive to depart from (3,3), the initial outcome is a nonmyopic equilibrium *for A.*

It is also a nonmyopic equilibrium for Player B. By symmetry, the calculus facing Player B at (3,3) is identical to that of A. And since neither player has a long-term incentive to move away from (3,3), this outcome is a nonmyopic equilibrium in this game.

It is important to point out that the compromise outcome is not the only nonmyopic equilibrium in Prisoners' Dilemma. The "noncooperative outcome" (2,2)—the unique Nash equilibrium and the conventional solution to this game—is also stable in the nonmyopic sense. If this outcome is the initial outcome, neither player would have an incentive to change his strategy because the player with the subsequent move would immediately terminate the process at the outcome best for him and worst for the departing player—at either (4,1) or (1,4).

More significant, however, is the fact that (2,2) is an "attractive" equilibrium in the sense of Fiorina and Shepsle (1982). This means that should any outcome other than (3,3) be the initial outcome, the process of alternating strategy choices will lead rationally to (2,2), where the move-countermove process will end, and not to (3,3). Hence, any oscillation, or even the appearance of movement from the status quo, implies (2,2) as the rational outcome of a game of mutual deterrence in its archetypical manifestation.[18]

Stable mutual deterrence in the game of figure 2.2, then, depends upon the transmission of tit-for-tat signals by both players to each other, that is, statements to the effect that each player intends to stick to his status-quo strategy as long as the other player does likewise, but that each player also intends to carry out his retaliatory threat should the other deviate from the status quo. In a sense, of course, such statements are implicit in the payoff structure of this game. Still, they must be reinforced so neither player suspects that the other plans to seek a temporary advantage by moving to his best outcome.

Nevertheless, the fact that a strategy supporting the "compromise" (3,3) outcome in a Prisoners' Dilemma game is both farsightedly rational and long-term stable means that there is no unavoidable conflict between the theory of mutual deterrence and the strictures of game theory. Moreover, provided that (3,3) is the initial outcome in this game, the rules (see above) that define the nonmyopic stability of this outcome can be considered sufficient conditions for the operation of deterrence in its prototypical form. In a subsequent section it will be seen that a specification of these rules is useful because it

18. Brams (1985) shows that when "two-sided" rationality is postulated, the deterrence equilibrium in Prisoners' Dilemma is also attractive. By contrast, the conflictual outcome is attractive in the absence of this assumption.

permits a logically consistent, and theoretically grounded, examination of the consequences for deterrence of departures from this ideal type.

2.4 Relaxing the Rules: The Concept of a Limited-Move Equilibrium

If the intersection of the structure of a Prisoners' Dilemma game and the rules that define a nonmyopic equilibrium constitute the ideal conditions for the operation of mutual deterrence, then, by relaxing either the rules or the structural characteristics of this game, the consequences of some typical departures from the prototype can be examined. Accordingly, in this section, I will explore the implications of some empirically plausible limitations on the ability of the players to make all of the logically possible moves and countermoves in a deterrence game. In the next section, I will similarly use the theory of moves to analyze the impact of different assumptions about the credibility of each player's retaliatory threat on the stability of the deterrence relationship.

It is not difficult to appreciate the fact that the rules that govern the ability of the players to make moves and countermoves in a sequential game may vary from one deterrence situation to another. For example, contrast for a moment the constraints that existed on decision-makers during the Cuban missile crisis of 1962 and the more recent conflict in the South Atlantic between Great Britain and Argentina over the Falkland Islands.[19] In the Cuban crisis, the outcome associated with mutual loss for the United States and the Soviet Union, (a_2,b_2), involved the very real possibility of a nuclear exchange. If this outcome had been reached in a sequence of moves and countermoves, it is likely that neither superpower would have had an opportunity to move *from it* to either (a_1,b_2)

19. Several competing game-theoretic explanations of the Cuban missile crisis can be found in Brams (1985), Howard (1971), and Snyder and Diesing (1977). A more detailed discussion of the Falkland crisis will be given in the next chapter.

or to (a_2,b_1). For all practical purposes, movement to (a_2,b_2) in the Cuban missile crisis implied termination of the game (and perhaps much more).

By contrast, in the Falkland crisis, both Britain and Argentina could, and apparently did, contemplate limited hostilities without the possibility of strategic retreat being foreclosed. In this case, movement *to*, and *through*, (a_2,b_2) seemed empirically possible. Thus, the ability of the players in each of these crises to make certain moves or countermoves was very different.

In addition to the possibility of some deterrence games exhibiting different rules governing moves and countermoves, it is also possible that different rules operate on various outcomes within the same game. In some games, a path from one outcome to another, involving several moves, may be open while a single move from another outcome may be blocked.[20] For instance, in the Cuban crisis, even though a single move from either (a_2,b_1) or (a_1,b_2) to (a_2,b_2) implied termination of the game, there is no compelling theoretical or empirical reason to believe that movement from, say, (a_2,b_1) to (a_1,b_1) to (a_1,b_2) was precluded.

The set of rules that govern the strategy choices of the players in a sequential game constitutes a continuum. At one end of this continuum is the rule (I) that limits the players to the minimum number of strategy choices in a game, that is, a single unilateral deviation from an outcome. Note that this rule defines the conditions associated with a Nash (or Type I) equilibrium.

At the other end of this continuum is the rule (IV) that permits the players to make the maximum number of moves and countermoves in a game (i.e., four, or two moves each) before cycling back to an initial outcome. Rule IV is the rule associated with the definition of a nonmyopic (or Type IV) equilibrium.[21]

---

20. An empirical example will be given in chapter 5.

21. Kilgour's (1984) generalization of this concept, called an *extended nonmyopic* (or *XNM*) equilibrium assumes that the players are able to make an unlimited number

In between these two extremes lie a number of other rules. But if one assumes that rules are symmetrical,[22] and that the players cannot backtrack or reverse a move,[23] then there are only two other points on the continuum of rules:

Rule II—where either player can make an initial move from a starting outcome or status-quo point and the other player can make one countermove, for a total of two possible moves. Outcomes that are stable when this rule is operative will be referred to as *Type II* equilibria.[24]

Rule III—where either player can make an initial move from a starting outcome *and* a single response to a counter-move of the other player, for a total of three possible moves. Outcomes that are stable under this rule will be referred to as *Type III* equilibria.

Since Type II and Type III equilibria are based on the idea that the players in a game are able to make more than the mini-mum, but less than the maximum, number of moves and countermoves, they are termed *limited-move* equilibria (Zagare 1984b). Such limited-move equilibria are appropriate mea-sures of outcome stability in dynamic games wherein the se-quential move process is fettered in some way, that is, in games

---

of moves and countermoves in a game, that is, are able to cycle indefinitely. This equi-librium concept, in essence, alters the initial definition of sequential play associated with the theory of moves (see rules 1 to 4 above) by extending the horizon of the play-ers outward. By contrast, the concept of a limited-move equilibrium, to be defined shortly, constricts these same rules to conform to the actuality of some real-world interactions.

22. This assumption will be relaxed in the next chapter when games of unilateral deterrence are examined.

23. This assumption will be relaxed in chapter 4 when the impact of power asym-metries is considered.

24. This rule, and its associated equilibrium concept, resembles the rule underly-ing the notion of a *Stackelberg equilibrium* which assumes that one player, the leader, makes his strategy choice in anticipation of the best response of the other player, the follower, while the follower merely reacts to the choice of the leader. (For a discus-sion, see Henderson and Quandt [1971, 229–31].) Rule II, by contrast, does not dis-tinguish different roles for the two players.

where it may not be possible for the players to either *get to* one outcome, or to *move through* another, or to *return to* still another. Thus, the concept of a limited-move equilibrium is a useful and necessary adjunct to the concept of a nonmyopic equilibrium and of the dynamic conception implied by the theory-of-moves framework, especially in empirical investigations where idiosyncratic features of real-life games might enter into the calculus of a player considering the long-term consequences of a strategy change. For while it is probably true that the assumption, defining a Nash equilibrium—that players are able to make only a single unilateral deviation from an outcome—is overly restrictive and not representative of the fluid nature of many deterrence situations, it is also probably true that the assumption, defining a nonmyopic equilibrium— that players can make an unlimited number of moves and countermoves—is frequently not satisfied in many empirical settings.[25] Therefore, in the subsequent analysis, but particularly in Part II of this book, each of these auxiliary equilibrium concepts will be called upon to gauge outcome stability whenever the appropriate limiting conditions (i.e., the rules associated with them) are of empirical or theoretical import. For now, however, I will digress briefly to describe the procedure for determining whether or not an outcome is a limited-move equilibrium of either type, and then explore the implications of these two different sets of constraints for the stability of mutual deterrence in its prototypical manifestation.

With one exception, the same backwards induction process that was used to determine nonmyopic stability can also be used to identify limited-move equilibria. The only difference is the length of the game tree. To determine whether or not an outcome is a nonmyopic equilibrium, a tree containing at least four moves away from an initial outcome must be used. By contrast, the test for Type II stability requires a tree of two

---

25. For an interesting and insightful comparison of these and related equilibrium concepts in terms of the ability of players to anticipate different moves and countermoves in a sequential game, see Kilgour (1985).

moves,[26] and the test for Type III stability requires a tree of
three moves, away from the status quo. Thus, to determine
whether (3,3) is a Type III limited-move equilibrium in Prisoners' Dilemma, a truncated version of the tree of figure 2.3
would be used, and the backward induction process would
commence with A's move at (2,2). Similarly, Type II stability
can be discerned by truncating the tree even further and beginning the backward induction process with B's choice at (4,1).

Using these procedures, it is easy to demonstrate that, in addition to being a nonmyopic (or Type IV) equilibrium, the
status quo (3,3) in Prisoners' Dilemma is also a Type II and a
Type III equilibrium.[27] But note that it is not a Nash (or Type I)
equilibrium. What this means is that the dynamic stability of
the status quo in this game depends upon the ability of both
players to *move to* (2,2). Since it is precisely the threat to move
to (2,2) that removes the incentive of the opponent to move
from (3,3), deterrence is likely to fail in this game if the ability
of either player to carry out this threat is problematic. In other
words, at the strategic level, a capable and credible retaliatory
threat is not sufficient to ensure stability. Successful deterrence
of a nuclear attack also depends upon each player's possession
of an invulnerable second-strike capability.

2.5 Other Mutual Deterrence Games

As previously indicated, the stability of the deterrence relationship depends not only on the characteristics of the rules
that govern the ability of the players to make moves and countermoves, but also on the particular configuration of player preferences over the set of possible outcomes. In this section,
therefore, I will examine the dynamics of mutual deterrence
when (a) neither player prefers to punish the unilateral departure of the other, and (b) when only one player prefers to ex-

26. For an example, see figure 5.3.
27. For the specifics of this calculation, but in terms of the game of Chicken, see
Zagare (1984b).

ecute the threat following the other's departure from the status quo. In chapter 3, I will explore the strategic implications of one player's preference for the status quo over all other outcomes. The following discussion, as before, assumes intersubjective agreement by the players about the nature of their threats, whatever the objective reality may be.

Neither Player Prefers to Punish the Other's Departure from the Status Quo

When both players prefer, or are seen to prefer, the other's departure from the status quo to the outcome associated with the execution of the deterrent threat, the game is "Chicken" (see figure 2.4). Chicken satisfies the restrictions of equations [2.3], [2.4], and [2.5], but not those of equation [2.6]. This means that in Chicken each player has a capable, but not a credible, retaliatory threat. Parenthetically, the Berlin crisis of 1948 is an example of a game with the structural characteristics of Chicken.

Interestingly, in Chicken, as in Prisoners' Dilemma, where a balance of credibility also exists, the status quo is both a non-myopic and a Type III limited-move equilibrium. However, because (3,3) is *not* a Type II equilibrium in Chicken, the conditions upon which the long-term stability of deterrence rests in this game are different than those of Prisoners' Dilemma. Indeed, the different stability characteristics of the status quo in Chicken have some very important implications for the functioning of deterrence in this game.

Recall that since the status quo is a Type II equilibrium in Prisoners' Dilemma, the long-term stability of (3,3) rests upon the ability of each player to *get to* (2,2). Thus, if either player's ability to inflict harm on the other were to be jeopardized by the other's departure from the status quo, deterrence would not be stable.

By contrast, the requirements for the long-term stability of the status quo in Chicken are more stringent. Here, stable

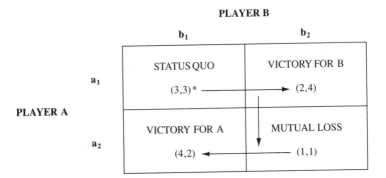

Key: * = nonmyopic equilibrium

FIGURE 2.4: Chicken

deterrence depends upon the ability of both players to *get
through* (a_2, b_2). To see this, consider the consequences of a
move by B from (3,3) to (2,4) in figure 2.4. If moves are un-
constrained, and backtracking is not permitted, A can eliminate B's incentive to move to (2,4) by threatening to move to
(1,1) and forcing B to accept (4,2), which B does not prefer to
the original status quo of (3,3). (See the arrows in figure 2.4.)

But consider now the calculus of the players if movement to
(1,1) implies the end of the game, as might be the case in nuclear Chicken, or even its teenage analogue. In this case, B
would have an incentive to move to (2,4) precisely because A
could not impose (4,2) on B by moving to (1,1). By symmetry,
under these conditions, A would also have an incentive to
move away from (3,3) in Chicken.

One implication of all of this is that at the strategic level,
under conditions of mutual fear, the stability of deterrence
rests upon the ability of the players to pass through or endure
mutual punishment, that is, to fight a limited war. To the extent
that carefully controlled levels of escalation are not possible,
deterrence is not stable when neither player has a credible retaliatory threat.

PLAYER B

	b_1	b_2
a_1	STATUS QUO (3,3) ——————→	VICTORY FOR B (2,4)*
a_2	VICTORY FOR A (4,1)	MUTUAL LOSS (1,2)

PLAYER A

Key: * = nonmyopic equilibrium

FIGURE 2.5: Called Bluff

Only One Player Prefers to Punish a Unilateral Departure from the Status Quo

If one player, say B, but not the other prefers to carry out his deterrent threat given a departure from the status quo by his opponent, the game depicted in figure 2.5 results. This game, dubbed "Called Bluff" by Snyder and Diesing (1977, 46), is a hybrid of the previous two since the preferences of the player who prefers to carry out his retaliatory threat are the same as those of each player in Prisoners' Dilemma, whereas the preferences of the other player are the same as each player's preferences in Chicken. As will be demonstrated presently, the name of this game is suggestive of its dynamics since each player has a capable threat, as defined by equations [2.4] and [2.5], but only one player's threat (i.e., B's), is credible, that is, satisfies the requirements of equation [2.6].

If the game is Called Bluff, mutual deterrence is not stable and is likely to fail.[28] The slight alteration of one player's preferences that induces this game provides the other player—the player willing to execute the threat—with a long-term incen-

28. For a more formal demonstration, see section 6.2.

tive to move from (3,3) to (2,4) (see the arrow in figure 4).[29] Moreover, since (2,4) is a nonmyopic equilibrium in this game, once this outcome is reached, neither player has an incentive to change his strategy again.[30] Thus, in Called Bluff, the player who is willing, and able, to punish the other, wins.[31]

2.6 Summary and Conclusions

In this chapter I examined the prototypical structure of the relationship of mutual deterrence and found that there is a natural congruence between this structure and that of Prisoners' Dilemma, a notorious game generally believed to impose suboptimal outcomes on those who play it. I offered some possible explanations for the failure of deterrence theorists to make this connection explicit in their expositions of the theory, and showed that this apparent anomaly can be reconciled with the logic of game theory by embedding the theory of deterrence within a dynamic framework called the theory of moves. More specifically, I showed that a strategy supporting a Pareto-optimal status-quo outcome is both long-term stable and far-sightedly rational, *provided that this outcome is the initial outcome and that both players have the ability to punish a defection from it by the other.*

Some typical departures from the ideal type of mutual deterrence were also examined in this chapter, and some interesting conclusions were drawn from this analysis. For instance, when one player is seen to prefer not to punish the other's unilateral defection from the status quo, deterrence is not stable. But curiously, when this preference is symmetrical, stable mutual deterrence is reestablished, although the stability of deter-

29. Since (3,3) is also not a Nash equilibrium, this player also has a *short-term* incentive to move to (2,4).
30. Since (2,4) is also a Nash equilibrium, neither player has a short-term incentive to change his strategy either.
31. The effect of repeated play for this result, discussed in the context of the Polish strategic situation of 1980–81, is analyzed by Brams and Hessel (1984).

rence in this case depends upon the ability of both players to pass through or endure mutual punishment, as in a limited war.

These conclusions are subject to many qualifications and provisos. Still, they suggest that the deterrence relationship is not as simple as some analysts have concluded. For example, Organski and Kugler (1980) note that strategic deterrence rests upon each player's fear of the other's nuclear capability. They also argue that a "necessary condition for the theory of deterrence to be valid, in cases where both sides have nuclear weapons, is that the competing nations react to one another" (Organski and Kugler 1980, 180). And, after offering evidence that there has been no connection between the arms acquisition process in the United States and the Soviet Union, they conclude that the "logical conditions for deterrence are absent, and . . . that mutual deterrence is not taking place" (Organski and Kugler 1980, 199).

But in light of the above, it is clear that too much fear is destabilizing. In nuclear Chicken, at least, when both players fear mutual punishment, or give the appearance of fearing it, deterrence is not stable. In Prisoners' Dilemma, though, where the opposite conditions hold and the players are unafraid of each other, as would be the case in the absence of a superpower arms race, mutual deterrence is stable. Thus, if correct, Organski and Kugler's empirical finding that a United States–Soviet Union arms race does not exist explains, rather than disconfirms, the stability of the superpower relationship and can be viewed as corroborating evidence for the arguments contained in this chapter.[32]

If, as postulated, the success of mutual deterrence is linked to the structure of a Prisoners' Dilemma game, then one would expect that players interested in deterrence would actively seek to devise games of this genre. There is also some evidence that supports this proposition. For instance, in chapters 5 and 6, I

32. For similar conclusions about the superpower arms race, see Wohlstetter (1974a, 1974b) and Allison and Morris (1976).

will demonstrate that American and Soviet decision-makers consciously attempted to create or reinforce the structure of a Prisoners' Dilemma game during the 1967 and 1973 crises in the Middle East. And Walker (1977, 157) shows that a connection existed between Henry Kissinger's "operational code" which "approximate[s] game theory's 'prisoner's dilemma' description of the nature of politics" and the bargaining behavior of the United States in Vietnam from 1969 to 1973. Snyder and Diesing's (1977, 497) finding that of the sixteen international crises in their data set the only "two crises that ended in more or less even compromise were both Prisoner's Dilemma" games is also consistent with the analysis contained in this chapter.[33]

33. For experimental evidence showing that players in Prisoners' Dilemma games tend to cooperate more frequently than one might expect, see Rapoport, Guyer, and Gordon (1976), Colman (1982), and the literature cited therein.

3

The Dynamics of
Unilateral Deterrence

In chapter 2 I used the theory of moves to examine the dynamics of mutual deterrence. In that chapter, not only were the conditions for the successful operation of mutual deterrence in its ideal manifestation identified, but the ramifications of some reasonable and empirically meaningful deviations from the prototype were also explored. In this chapter I shall extend the previous analysis to the case of *unilateral* deterrence, which I define to be a deterrence situation wherein a satisfied, status-quo power is pitted against an unsatisfied revisionist state.[1] Curiously, this extension is not as straightforward as might be expected. In the unilateral deterrence relationship, an instability problem not present in a relationship of mutual deterrence arises unexpectedly. As a result, the ability of a status-quo nation to deter a revisionist state in these games is rendered problematic.

To demonstrate this problem, and to offer an understanding of the conditions under which it might be circumvented, I will begin with a brief description of the Falkland/Malvinas crisis of 1982, a game that illustrates what I call the "pathology" of unilateral deterrence. In the next section, I will introduce another set of stability criteria drawn from the theory of moves and interpret the implications of these criteria for the functioning of deterrence in its unilateral variant. Finally, I discuss the implications for the stability of unilateral-deterrence relation-

1. This chapter is based upon Frank C. Zagare, "The Pathologies of Unilateral Deterrence," in Urs Luterbacher and Michael D. Ward, eds., *Dynamic Models of International Conflict* (Boulder, Colo.: Lynne Rienner Publishers, 1985).

ships of the inability of the players to make certain kinds of moves in a sequential game.

3.1 The Pathology of Unilateral Deterrence

To illustrate the problems implicit in the dynamics of unilateral-deterrence relationships, consider for now the strategic situation, as the regime of Argentinian President Leopoldo Galtieri probably perceived it, immediately preceding the Falkland/Malvinas crisis of 1982. The strategies, outcomes, and the postulated preferences of the two players in the putative game the Argentinian leadership thought it was playing with the British are summarized in figure 3.1. In this representation, the British are assumed to have two major options, either to fortify and defend the Falkland Islands or not to fortify them and leave the islands exposed to possible military action

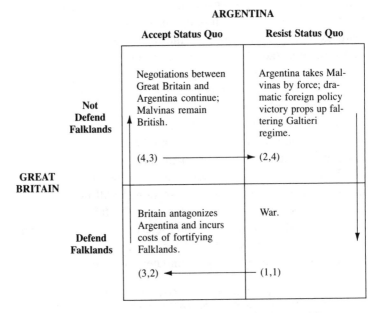

FIGURE 3.1: Outcome Matrix of the Falkland-Malvinas Crisis of 1982

by Argentina. For their part, the Argentinians are assumed to have a choice between accepting the (pre-invasion) status quo, i.e., continuing British sovereignty (or de facto control if a leasing agreement or some other face-saving device could be negotiated) or using force to upset the long-standing British control of the Malvinas.

As before, the preferences of the players are represented by the ordered pair in each cell of the outcome matrix, and are ranked from best to worst, with each player's best outcome represented by a "4," each player's next-best outcome represented by a "3," and so on. Two of the assumptions about these postulated preferences deserve particular comment. First, since the Galtieri regime clearly did not want to fight for the Malvinas, and since it did not expect the British to "go to war for such a small problem as these few rocky islands" (Haig 1984, 287), the outcome associated with mutual punishment (i.e., war) is assumed to be the worst outcome for both states. This interpretation of the preferences of the two players is consistent with most evaluations of this crisis prior to the actual outbreak of hostilities. As *Time* (April 19, 1982, p. 28) put it two weeks before the British invaded Port Stanley, "the looming war" in the southeast Atlantic "was one that neither Britain nor Argentina wanted or could afford." [In terms of the definitions offered in chapter 2, neither player is assumed to have an inherently credible threat. Later, this assumption will be shown to be inconsequential to the analysis of this game.] And second, note that in this representation of the Falkland/Malvinas crisis, the British are assumed to prefer the existing status quo to all other outcomes, making this a game of unilateral, rather than mutual, deterrence.

The major pathology of unilateral deterrence relationships is manifest in the Falkland/Malvinas game of figure 3.1: the status quo (4,3) is not stable in either the long-term, or nonmyopic, sense or even in the short-term sense of Nash. The fundamental instability of the status-quo outcome, therefore, renders problematic unilateral deterrence in this and—as will be seen—similar games.

The reason why the status quo is not a nonmyopic equilibrium in this game is that there is no *termination* of the sequence of moves and countermoves, as there was in each of the mutual deterrence games discussed in chapter 2. More specifically, given a move away from (4,3) by the Argentinian government, neither player has an opportunity to terminate the game by stopping at its best outcome. Put in a slightly different way, the move and countermove process in the Falkland/Malvinas game is cyclic,[2] that is, at least one player has an incentive to move from *every* outcome, as indicated by the arrows in figure 3.1. Moreover, since this game lacks a nonmyopic equilibrium, explanations and predictions about it are rendered problematic. In other words, this game, as presently formulated, is *indeterminate*.[3]

Significantly, this conclusion would not be affected in any way if the credibility assumptions reflected in figure 3.1—neither player's threat is assumed to be credible—are altered. The status-quo outcome in each of the unilateral-deterrence games listed in figure 3.2, games 64(48) and 15(21), in which the revisionist player is assumed to have a credible threat, are also not nonmyopic or Nash equilibria. The same is also true of the two games listed in figure 3.3, games 76(72) and 65(55), in which the revisionist player is assumed not to have a credible threat.[4] (Ignore, for now, the arrows in these figures.) In addition, *no outcome* in all four of these games is a nonmyopic equilibrium.[5]

2. For a more extensive discussion of this point, see Brams and Wittman (1981).

3. It should be pointed out that (2,4) is a Nash equilibrium in the Falkland-Malvinas game of figure 3.1. However, the ability of Nash's equilibrium concept to explain either the dynamics or the eventual outcome of this game is clearly inadequate.

4. Unlike the games discussed in chapter 2, the four core games of unilateral deterrence depicted in figures 3.2 and 3.3 have no particular names. In at least two taxonomies, however, the 78 distinct 2 × 2 games have been assigned numbers. The two numbers for each game given in these figures are the numbers assigned by Brams (1977) (the first number) and by Rapoport and Guyer (1966) (the number in parentheses).

5. Game 65(55) in figure 3.3 is the same as the Falkland-Malvinas game of figure 3.1. It is reproduced here to facilitate the subsequent discussion.

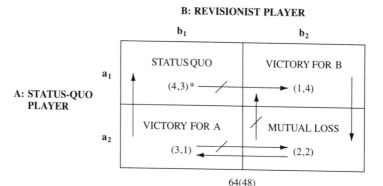

Key: * = absorbing outcome

FIGURE 3.2: Two Unilateral Deterrence Games. The Threat of the Revisionist Player Is Assumed to Be Credible.

3.2 Two Questions About Unilateral Deterrence

In the previous section, an essential indeterminacy was shown to characterize the four core games of unilateral deterrence. Without additional assumptions, therefore, not only is it difficult to say whether or not deterrence will succeed (i.e., is

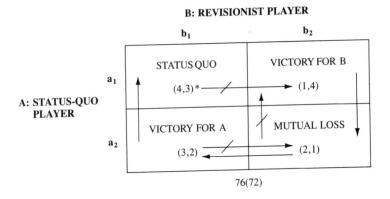

76(72)

65(55)

Key: * = absorbing outcome

FIGURE 3.3: Two Unilateral Deterrence Games. The Threat of the Revisionist Player Is Not Assumed to Be Credible.

stable) in these games, but it is also difficult to specify what outcome will evolve if and when deterrence fails.[6]

6. It should be pointed out that the (2,4) outcomes associated with a victory for the revisionist player in both games 15(21) and 65(55) are Nash equilibria, since neither player has an *immediate* incentive to move, unilaterally, from it. Thus, even though both of these equilibrium concepts coincide in their evaluation that unilateral deterrence is unstable in these two games, Nash's equilibrium concept predicts a victory for the revisionist player. By contrast, the concept of a nonmyopic equilibrium

It is especially important to note that the indeterminacy endemic to unilateral-deterrence games can be directly attributed to the fact that one player in each game prefers the status quo to all other outcomes. Were the preference ranking of the status-quo player's two best outcomes simply reversed, making each of these games a game of mutual deterrence, one outcome in each game would be singled out as a nonmyopic equilibrium. More specifically, given the provisos mentioned in the previous chapter, in two of the four transformed games— 64(48) and 65(55)—deterrence is stable since it is the status quo that is converted into a nonmyopic equilibrium by this preference alteration. By contrast, in the two remaining games in which only one player has a credible threat—15(21) and 76(72)—deterrence is not stable; in each of these games, the unique nonmyopic equilibrium is associated with the best outcome of the player with, and the next-worst outcome of the player without, a credible threat.

At this point, there are two obvious questions. First, what additional assumptions are necessary to render determinate the four games of unilateral deterrence? And second, given that such conditions can be identified, will deterrence succeed or fail in these four games? In what follows, two different sets of stability criteria,[7] one new and one not, drawn from the theory of moves will be discussed and their implications for the stability of deterrence in the unilateral case explored.[8]

---

admits the possibility of a move to an immediately less attractive outcome [i.e., (a_2, b_2)] by the status-quo player in order ultimately to induce an outcome better than $(2,4)$ for the status-quo player. In other words, the concept of a nonmyopic equilibrium reveals a "long-term" instability in the $(2,4)$ outcomes in both of these games.

7. Another set, associated with the concept of "holding power," will be introduced in chapter 4.

8. Note that although the nature of this problem is somewhat different from the kind of indeterminacy discussed in chapter 1, i.e., the indeterminacy associated with multiple nonequivalent or noninterchangeable equilibria, it has similar theoretical implications and is just as pernicious. More specifically, unless competing equilibria can be eliminated in those games with multiple equilibria, or unless some equilibrium can be found where none ostensively exist, explanations and predictions based upon game-theoretic models will be deficient.

3.3 The Absorbing Criteria and Attitudes Toward Risk

One set of conditions sufficient to induce a determinate outcome in each of the four core games of unilateral deterrence is associated with the concept of an *absorbing outcome* found in Brams and Hessel (1982). The stability attributes reflected in the concept of an absorbing outcome rest upon the supposition that in a 2 × 2 game without a nonmyopic equilibrium, where at least one player has an incentive to move away from every outcome, the incentive to move from some outcomes will be stronger than the incentive to move away from others. As will be seen, the nature of these incentives has some important implications for the stability of the status quo in unilateral-deterrence games.

To demonstrate this, assume (1) that players will always move away from their worst and next-worst outcomes, and (2) that when there is a conflict between these two norms, a player will not move from that outcome that leads to a better outcome than the other. Given these two assumptions, at least one outcome in 33 of the 41 distinct 2 × 2 games without a nonmyopic equilibrium is considered to be an absorbing outcome. As its name suggests, such an outcome, will, like a black hole, attract movement toward itself. Consequently, if an absorbing outcome is either the initial outcome, or if it is reached in a sequence of moves and countermoves, it will exhibit a degree of stability absent in outcomes that are not absorbing. For this reason, Brams and Hessel (1982, 394) characterize absorbing outcomes as " 'conditionally' or 'almost nonmyopically' stable."

The two assumptions—(1) and (2)—mentioned in the preceding paragraph are not sufficient to induce an absorbing outcome in any of the four unilateral-deterrence games discussed herein. Moreover, as the arrows in figures 3.2 and 3.3 indicate (ignore for now the slashes indicating the *deletion* of some of the arrows), a cycle would still exist among the four outcomes in each game even if it were assumed (3) that a player would move from his next-best outcome (i.e., "3"). In other words, given assumptions (1) through (3), the process of moves and countermoves remains intransitive in these four games.

In order for an absorbing outcome to be induced in the four core games of unilateral deterrence, assumption (3) must be relaxed and replaced with assumption (4), that a player will consider moving from his next-best outcome unless, by not moving, he can break the cycle and thereby assure himself of an outcome that exceeds his *security level,* that is, an outcome that is at least as good as his next best.[9] For each of the four unilateral-deterrence games, then, assumption (4) is both necessary and sufficient to render one outcome—significantly the status-quo outcome, (4,3)—an absorbing outcome. Moreover, underscoring the essential familial relationship among these four games is the fact that, given assumption (4), they *uniquely* constitute one of the four distinct categories of 2×2 games with an absorbing outcome.

In order to demonstrate the above, consider now the arrows in game 64(48) in figure 3.2. The six arrows in this, and the remaining three, games of figures 3.2 and 3.3 are implied by assumptions (1) through (3) that players will consider moving from their worst, next-worst, and next-best outcomes. As the arrows indicate, these assumptions lead to a cycle among the four outcomes.

Now, assume (4) that the revisionist player would be satisfied with his next-best outcome rather than risk cycling in order to obtain his best outcome. In this case, the arrow from (4,3) to (1,4) can be *deleted*—deleted arrows are indicated by a slash through them. But the deletion of this arrow logically

9. A player's security level for a game is defined to be the best outcome he can assure himself of. For instance, in game 76(72), the status-quo player can guarantee a payoff of at least "2", i.e., his next-worst, by selecting his non-status-quo strategy, (a_2). Thus "2" represents the security level of the revisionist player in this game. For similar reasons, "2" represents the security level of both players in each of the four core games of unilateral deterrence examined herein. Note, however, that in some games, a player might have a higher security level. The coincidence of security levels in each of these games is just that.

implies the deletion of both the arrow away from (3,1) leading to (2,2) and the deletion of the arrow away from (2,2) leading to (1,4).

Briefly, the rational for the deletion of the two arrows is as follows. Suppose the process of moves and countermoves reaches (3,1). At (3,1), as the arrows indicate, both players have an incentive to move to another outcome. But the fact that (4,3) is acceptable to the revisionist player—see assumption (4)—means that the revisionist player would prefer not to move to (2,2) in order to induce his best outcome at (1,4) from which a cycle is still possible, but instead would prefer that the status-quo player be the one to move, away from (3,1) to (4,3), and thereby induce the next-best outcome of the revisionist player. Hence, given the deletion of the arrow at (4,3), the deletion of the arrow from (3,1) to (2,2) is also implied.

Similar logic leads to the deletion of the arrow from (2,2) to (1,4). Given the deletion of the arrow from (4,3), the status-quo player would prefer a move by the revisionist player to (3,1) that would, in turn, lead rationally to his best outcome at (4,3), to his own move from (2,2) that would lead to his worst outcome at (1,4).

Notice that with the deletion of these two additional arrows, the remaining arrows all lead to, or *converge upon,* (4,3). This means that if one assumes that the revisionist player has an aversion to cycling, then the outcome implied by a sequence of moves and countermoves, no matter what outcome is the starting outcome, is (4,3). Put in a slightly different way, the assumption that the revisionist player prefers not to cycle is sufficient to induce the stability of the status quo in this, and the remaining three, games of unilateral deterrence.[10]

How reasonable is this assumption? It is difficult to say, especially given the ordinal framework assumed in this analysis. Under some circumstances, cycling may indeed be rational, in an expected value sense, depending upon each player's cardinal

10. For an empirical example, see section 6.4.

evaluation of the outcomes and his estimate of the probability that each of the four outcomes will be selected as the final outcome of the game. On the other hand, depending upon these same factors, cycling might produce a lower expected payoff than that associated with the certain selection of the status-quo outcome.

Patently, however, in such a situation, cycling will have a higher expected payoff, ceteris paribus, the more intense the preferences of the revisionist player for his best outcome. Conversely, the expected value of precipitating a cycle will be diminished for a player who places a relatively low evaluation on his worst or next-worst outcome. This suggests that the attitude of the revisionist player toward risk is a key determinant of the stability of deterrence in the unilateral case. Risk-averse actors, with deflated evaluations of their best outcome relative to the other outcomes, will most likely find the status quo acceptable. By contrast, unilateral deterrence is more problematic when the revisionist player, with more intense preferences, is risk-acceptant.[11] Unfortunately, the failure of deterrence that produced the brief war between Great Britain and Argentina in 1982 is probably testimony to this fact.

3.4 The Impact of Nuclear Weapons

To some, the implications of the preceding analysis may have been encouraging. After all, if nothing else, nuclear weapons probably inspire risk-aversion among leaders of revisionist states faced with the dire consequences of nuclear retaliation.[12] Unfortunately, the conclusion that such weapons of mass destruction are necessarily conducive to unilateral-deterrence stability is unwarranted. It is unwarranted not because these weapons lead to a "competition in risk taking"

11. According to Brams (1976, 63), "risk acceptance and preference intensity are simply two different ways to describe the same phenomenon."

12. Otherwise, as Bueno de Mesquita's (1985a, 168–69) data suggest, they are probably risk-neutral.

rather than to an aversion to cycling, but because, if used, they may foreclose the possibility of cycling altogether.

It has not always been so. For example, as Quester (1970, 25) has argued, had the United States been a status-quo power in 1945 and hence, content "with pushing the Nazi regime back within its own boundaries," a return to a prewar status quo after a major-power conflict was conceivable. By contrast, it is difficult to imagine that any political and social system could survive the devastating consequences of an all-out nuclear war.

The environmental consequences of nuclear weapons, of course, go even further than this. Not only may they preclude returning to some outcome after it has been left, but they may also foreclose the possibility of moving through or even getting to other outcomes. As noted earlier, in situations such as these, where particular features of the real world fetter the sequential move process, the concept of a limited-move equilibrium is an appropriate gauge of outcome stability. Accordingly, using this concept as a guide, I will now briefly discuss the implications of five different sets of empirically plausible constraints for the stability of unilateral deterrence. These results are summarized in table 3.1.

1. *Both Players Possess First-Strike Capability.* When both players possess a first-strike capability, each player is, in effect, limited to a single, unilateral deviation from the status quo, and the stability requirements reduce to those associated with the concept of a Nash equilibrium. The Nash criteria, therefore, define one extreme of the continuum of move limitations and, as previously noted, the criteria that define a nonmyopic equilibrium represent the other extreme.

Since the status quo in each of the four unilateral-deterrence games is neither a Nash nor a nonmyopic equilibrium, there is no stability at either extreme. At least one player (i.e., the revisionist player) will always have an incentive, unilaterally, to depart from the status quo. But when both players have a first-strike capability, even the status-quo player will have such an

TABLE 3.1: Stability Implications of Move Limitations in Unilateral Deterrence Games

	Both players have a credible threat; game 64(48)	Status-quo player has a credible threat; game 76(72)	Neither player has a credible threat; game 65(55)	Revisionist player has a credible threat; game 15(21)
Both Players have only a first-strike capability	Unstable deterrence: both players have an incentive to preempt			
Revisionist player has a first- and a second-strike capability	Unstable deterrence: both players have an incentive to preempt			Revisionist player wins
Status-quo player has a first- and a second-strike capability	Stable deterrence	Stable deterrence	Unstable deterrence: both players have an incentive to preempt	Revisionist player wins
MAD: both have a second-strike capability	Stable deterrence	Stable deterrence	Unstable deterrence; both preempt	Revisionist player wins
War fighting	Stable deterrence			Revisionist player wins

incentive. By preempting the move of the revisionist player, and moving from his best outcome (a_1,b_1) to his next-best outcome (a_2,b_1), the status-quo player is able to avoid either his worst or his next-worst outcome which would be induced should the revisionist player strike first. Clearly, deterrence is extremely unstable—and unlikely—under these conditions.

2. *The Revisionist Player Has a First- and Second-Strike Capability.* The revisionist player's first-strike capability—which precludes a second-strike capability for the status-quo player—means that he can preempt the move of the status-quo player and end the game at (a_1,b_2). His second-strike capability—which precludes a first-strike capability for the status-quo player—means that he can respond to a unilateral departure from (a_1,b_1) by the status quo player and induce—if he prefers—(a_2,b_2).

Unilateral deterrence is no less stable when the revisionist player has both a first- and second-strike capability. The revisionist player will *always* have an incentive to preempt, although the motivation of the status-quo player to attempt to preempt the move of the revisionist player is somewhat different. The status-quo player, as before, will have an incentive to move from his best outcome, in order to avoid his worst and next-worst outcomes, in the two games [65(55) and 76(72)] in which the revisionist player's threat to retaliate is not credible, and also in the one game [64(48)] in which he prefers mutual punishment to the victory of the revisionist player. But in game 15(21), where the status-quo player prefers the victory of the revisionist player to mutual punishment, and where the revisionist player's threat is credible, the status-quo player would prefer not to upset the status quo first. In effect, under these conditions, the status-quo player would surrender.

3. *The Status-Quo Player has a First- and Second-Strike Capability.*[13] The complete instability manifest in the previous

13. The most obvious historical analogue is the U.S.-USSR strategic relationship during the early 1960s. This relationship will be explored in chapter 7.

two cases is altered when it is the status-quo player, not the revisionist player, who has a first- and second-strike capability. When these conditions apply, a credible and a capable threat by the status-quo player is both necessary and sufficient for successful deterrence—see games 64(48) and 76(72). In the absence of such a threat—as in games 15(21) and 65(55)—the revisionist player will have an incentive to move from (a_1,b_1) in order to induce his best outcome at (a_1,b_2); similarly, the status-quo player will also have an incentive to preempt in order to avoid his next-worst outcome should the revisionist player move from the status quo first.

4. *Mutual Assured Destruction.* Under this set of constraints, both players are assumed to be able to *move to,* but *not through* (a_2,b_2), as might be the case in a conflict between two nuclear powers who anticipate that any confrontation will escalate into a nuclear war and termination of the game.[14] Such a situation differs from the previous case only by the assumption that the revisionist player also has a second-strike capability. Interestingly, however, save for one small exception, the strategic situation is the same in both cases. A credible threat on the part of the status-quo player remains a necessary and a sufficient condition for stable deterrence since the revisionist player retains an incentive to move from the status quo in its absence. But the status-quo player's incentive to preempt [i.e., game 15(22)] is removed when the revisionist player's threat to retaliate is credible. In this one game, the victory of the revisionist player is implied by the rules that limit the ability of the players to move or countermove. All in all, however, a second-strike capability for the revisionist player has a negligible effect on the dynamics of unilateral deterrence.

5. *War Fighting.* Under this set of constraints, both players are assumed to have a war-fighting capability, that is, the ability to *get through* (a_2,b_2), the outcome associated with mutual punishment, but are assumed to not be able to *return to* (a_1,b_1),

14. This set of constraints defines Type II limited-move equilibria.

the original status quo.[15] Hence, movement from the status quo implies, depending upon the preferences of the players, a victory for one player or the other after a brief confrontation, or prolonged conflict at (a_2,b_2).

Notice that when these conditions are satisfied, either player is limited to an initial move from the status quo and a single response to the countermove of the other. Thus, the choice of whether the sequential move process *moves to* (a_2,b_2) rests with the player who does not choose, initially, to upset the status quo; and the choice of whether the process *moves through* (a_2,b_2) is up to the player who moves from the status quo first.

Significantly, the ability of both players to get through (a_2,b_2), coupled with the inability to return to (a_1,b_1), renders deterrence stable in three of the four games of unilateral deterrence examined herein. A credible threat by the status-quo player is no longer a necessary condition for stable unilateral deterrence, though it remains a sufficient condition. The lack of a credible threat by the revisionist player is also a sufficient condition for stability in these games. Unilateral deterrence is unstable only in game 15(21) wherein the revisionist player, but not the status-quo player, has a credible threat. In this game, the victory of the revisionist player at (a_1,b_2) is implied by the rules that preclude movement back to the status quo, regardless of which player upsets it first.

3.5 Summary and Conclusions

The theory-of-moves framework is used in this chapter to explore the dynamics of unilateral deterrence, wherein a satisfied status-quo state is pitted against an unsatisfied revisionist power. Four games typical of this type of relationship are identified. Because each of these games lacks a nonmyopic equilibrium, it is argued that they are essentially indeterminate. Consequently, without qualifying assumptions, little can be said about either the probability that unilateral deterrence will

---

15. This set of constraints defines Type III limited-move equilibria.

succeed, or the likely consequence of a breakdown of deterrence in these games.

To induce more determinate results, two sets of stability criteria, drawn from the theory of moves, were introduced, and their impact on the stability of unilateral deterrence in the unilateral case examined. Each set of postulates was shown to have a variable effect on the unilateral-deterrence relationship.

The stability criteria associated with the notion of an absorbing outcome were examined first. Underscoring the essential relationship among the four key games of unilateral deterrence is the fact that they uniquely constitute one of the four distinguishable categories of games with an absorbing outcome. Significantly, the status-quo outcome in each of these games is rendered stable in the absorbing sense if the revisionist player is risk-averse, that is, prefers to accept his next-best outcome to risking a cycle in order to induce his best outcome. In the absence of this assumption, however, the four unilateral-deterrence games examined in this chapter remain indeterminate.

The second set of rationality postulates explored in this chapter is associated with the concept of a limited-move equilibrium, or an outcome that is stabilized when environmental factors preclude players in a sequential game from making all of the logically possible moves and countermoves. Given the essentially idiosyncratic nature of such move limitations, only a selected number of empirically plausible constraints were examined. In general, this analysis revealed that the lack of limitations on the ability of the players to move from one outcome to another tended to foster, rather than destroy, the possibility of stable unilateral deterrence.

At the most extreme end of the continuum, when either the revisionist player alone, or both players simultaneously, have a first-strike capability, deterrence is very unstable. Under these conditions, in all but one possible situation, both players have an incentive to launch a preemptive assault on the other. Stability begins to emerge in these games when the status-quo player has both a second-strike capability and a credible retaliatory threat. Finally, provided that a return to the status quo ante is not possible, unilateral deterrence is stable in three of the four core games when the players have the ability to pass through the outcome associated with mutual punishment.

One interesting conclusion that can be drawn from an analysis of move limitations on the unilateral-deterrence relationship concerns the overall destabilizing impact of nuclear weapons. To the extent that such weapons are associated with a first-strike capability, or to the extent that they preclude carefully controlled levels of escalation (i.e., a war-fighting capability), nuclear weapons add little, and in some cases detract from, the possibility of deterrence in the unilateral case.

Other conclusions that derive from this analysis concern the general nature of the unilateral-deterrence relationship and the impact that a credible retaliatory threat has on it. The overall picture of unilateral deterrence that emerges from the analysis in this chapter is one of complexity and fragility. Slight alterations in parameters such as risk-taking propensities, and the ability of players to move to, get through, or return to, certain outcomes were shown to have important implications for the possibility of unilateral deterrence. Moreover, while a credible threat was seen to be an important part of the deterrence equation, it is, in general, neither a necessary nor a sufficient condition for the emergence of a strategic balance. Unilateral deterrence remains stable, even when the status-quo player lacks a credible retaliatory threat, as long as it is faced with a risk-averse revisionist player.

4

On Capability and Power

4.1 Capability

Up to this point, the dynamics of three mutual- and four unilateral-deterrence games have been explored. Except for the assumptions that separate unilateral- and mutual-deterrence relationships, these games are distinguished from one another only by different assumptions about the credibility of each player's retaliatory threat. Conspicuously absent from the analysis so far has been an evaluation of the role that capability plays in the deterrence relationship.

There is a very good reason for this: a capable threat is a *necessary* condition for deterrence against a revisionist player in either mutual- or unilateral-deterrence situations.[1] This means that in a game in which at least one player's threat lacks capability, deterrence will fail. Therefore, very little is added to an understanding of deterrence relationships by altering the assumption of capability.[2]

To see this, consider now the two mutual-deterrence games listed in figure 4.1. In both of these games, each player is dissatisfied with the prevailing status quo and prefers that the other player refrain from upsetting it. Moreover, in both games, each player has a credible threat, that is, prefers to resist, rather than accede to, a deviation from the status quo by his

1. By definition, all threats against a status-quo player are capable. Since such a player is assumed to prefer the status quo to all other outcomes, the restrictions of equation [2.5] are automatically satisfied.
2. As will be demonstrated shortly, this is not true when power asymmetries, as distinct from capabilities, are considered.

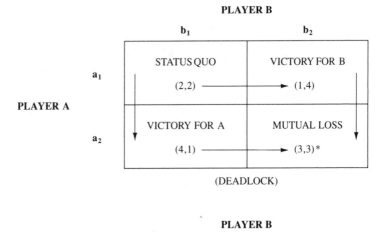

Key: * = nonmyopic equilibrium

FIGURE 4.1: Two Mutual Deterrence Games

opponent. These two games differ from one another only with respect to the assumptions they reflect about the capability of each player's retaliatory threat. In the first game, called "Deadlock" by Snyder and Diesing (1977, 45–46), since each player prefers mutual punishment to the existing status quo, each player's threat, while credible, is not capable. By contrast, in the second (Prisoners' Dilemma) game, since the restrictions of equation [2.5] are satisfied, each player has a capable threat.

As was demonstrated in chapter 2, mutual deterrence constitutes a stable relationship when both players have a credible and capable threat (in Prisoners' Dilemma) and, under certain conditions, may even remain stable when the credibility requirement is dropped for both players (in Chicken). By contrast, in Deadlock, all semblances of stability evaporate. In this game, it is rational to "suffer" the punishment rather than endure the indignities of the original status quo. Each player has an incentive to move away from the status quo and to respond to a unilateral deviation from it by his opponent. [See the arrows in figure 4.1.] Not surprisingly, therefore, the outcome associated with mutual punishment, (3,3), is the unique nonmyopic equilibrium in this game. Clearly, when both players are unable to punish one another, deterrence will fail.[3]

Moreover, this result is generalizable to all deterrence situations wherein an opponent of a revisionist player (in either a unilateral or mutual-deterrence situation) does not possess a capable threat. As can be seen from figures 4.2 and 4.3, the status quo, and hence deterrence, is not stable in each of the deterrence games that can be generated by altering the credibility assumptions of the player posited to lack capability (i.e., A). Of course, the eventual outcome of these interactions depends upon the preferences of Player A. When A lacks a credible threat and prefers not to resist B's departure from the status quo, as in games 11(17) and 35(35), a victory for B is implied. But when Player A's preferences for these two outcomes are reversed, as in games 20(11) and 45(46), conflict can be expected.

In this context, it will be instructive to contrast these conclusions with those derived from an expected utility analysis of the two games listed in figure 4.1. Consider, first, Deadlock.

It is easy to show that, in Deadlock, the expected utility of each player's nonstatus-quo strategy exceeds that of its status-

---

3. Snyder and Diesing (1977, 125) list the U.S.-Japanese relationship in 1940 as an empirical example of Deadlock.

PLAYER B

	b₁	b₂
a₁	STATUS QUO (3,2)	VICTORY FOR B (1,4)
a₂	VICTORY FOR A (4,1)	MUTUAL LOSS (2,3)*

PLAYER A is labeled to the left, between a₁ and a₂.

[20(11)]

PLAYER B

	b₁	b₂
a₁	STATUS QUO (3,2)	VICTORY FOR B (2,4)*
a₂	VICTORY FOR A (4,1)	MUTUAL LOSS (1,3)

[35(35)]

Key: * = nonmyopic equilibrium

FIGURE 4.2: Two Mutual Deterrence Games in Which One Player (A) Lacks a Capable Threat

quo supporting strategy. Hence, expected utility theory, in suggesting that conflict will occur, is completely congruent with the deductions generated by the theory of moves.

To demonstrate this,[4] assume that State A estimates that

4. Again, solely for the purposes of exposition and illustration, these ranks are treated as if they were cardinal utilities. The subsequent calculations, though, apply to any set of utilities that maintains the same ordinal relationship among the set of outcomes.

PLAYER B

	b₁	b₂
a₁	STATUS QUO (4,2)	VICTORY FOR B (2,4)*
a₂	VICTORY FOR A (3,1)	MUTUAL LOSS (1,3)

PLAYER A appears to the left of the rows a₁ and a₂.

[11(17)]

PLAYER B

	b₁	b₂
a₁	STATUS QUO (4,2)	VICTORY FOR B (1,4)
a₂	VICTORY FOR A (3,1)	MUTUAL LOSS (2,3)*

PLAYER A appears to the left of the rows a₁ and a₂.

[45(46)]

Key: * = absorbing outcome

FIGURE 4.3: Two Unilateral Deterrence Games in Which One Player (A) Lacks a Capable Threat

State B will select its status-quo strategy with some probability, p, and that it will challenge the status quo with probability $(1 - p)$. Hence, the expected utility for State A of its status-quo strategy, a_1, is:

$$E_A(a_1) = 2 (p) + 1 (1 - p). \qquad [4.1a]$$

And the expected utility for State A of its nonstatus-quo supporting strategy, (a_2), is:

$$E_A(a_2) = 4 (p) + 3 (1 - p). \qquad [4.1b]$$

Since $4 > 2$, the first factor of equation [4.1b] will always be larger than the first factor of equation [4.1a], no matter what value p takes on. And since $3 > 1$, the second factor of equation [4.1b] will always be larger than the second factor of equation [4.1a], no matter what value $(1 - p)$ takes on. Hence, $E_A(a_2) > E_A(a_1)$. By symmetry, $E_B(b_2) > E_B(b_1)$. Thus, both players have a higher expected utility in Deadlock for upsetting the status quo. An expected utility analysis, therefore, concurs with the perspective of the theory of moves in suggesting conflict.

All of this changes, however, when Prisoners' Dilemma is considered. In Prisoners' Dilemma,

$$E_A(a_1) = 3\,(p) + 1\,(1 - p), \text{ and} \qquad\qquad [4.2a]$$
$$E_A(a_2) = 4\,(p) + 2\,(1 - p). \qquad\qquad\qquad [4.2b]$$

By the same reasoning as above, $E_A(a_2) > E_A(a_1)$. And by symmetry, $E_B(b_2) > E_B(b_1)$. As before, both players have a higher expected utility for upsetting the status quo and, using an expected utility approach, one would predict conflict. By contrast, a theory-of-moves analysis reveals that deterrence constitutes a stable relationship in this game, provided that $(3,3)$ is the initial outcome and that both players have the ability to punish a defection from it by the other.

That expected utility models fail to discern the subtle structural differences between games like Deadlock and Prisoners' Dilemma is one reason why they can provide only the necessary, but not the sufficient, conditions for interstate conflict (see, for instance, Bueno de Mesquita 1982, 1985a). In other words, because these models tend to suppress important relational characteristics of some interactions, they will, by necessity, tend to overpredict the outbreak of war. Moreover, as was demonstrated in chapter 1, because expected utility models fail to take cognizance of the impact of utility interdependencies on rational choice, they are unable to explain anomalous cases such as the use of threats or an actual intervention when the expected utility of both actors for conflict is lower than the expected utility of their cooperative strategies (Guetzkow 1982; Zagare 1982b).[5]

4.2 Holding Power

Related to, but distinct from, the concept of capability is the concept of "power." As indicated in chapter 1, there is probably no more contentious concept in political science than power. Thus it should not be surprising that even within the theory-of-moves framework, several different definitions of power exist. Of these, the notion of *holding power* is most relevant to a discussion of deterrence in games played just one time.[6]

Consistent with Deutsch's (1978, 23) definition that power is "the ability to prevail in conflict," the concept of holding power starts with the assumption that a more powerful player with holding power, (H), has the ability of remaining at an outcome in a sequential game *longer* than the player without holding power, (NH). Thus, depending upon the preferences of the two players, H might be able to force NH to backtrack and thereby induce a better outcome than would arise if the sequential move process were strictly alternating. In other words, the range of choices open to a player with holding power is assumed to be expanded. While NH, as before, can choose to either stay at, or move from, each outcome when it is his turn to make a move, H, after a preliminary choice of moving or

---

5. This is in no way meant to demean the very real accomplishments of this school. Rather, it is to suggest that sounder explanations and predictions require a more explicit interactive component than that provided by expected-utility models alone.

6. For the effect of "moving power," or the ability of one player to move indefinitely after the other player is forced to stop after some finite number of moves, see Brams (1983). And Brams and Hessel (1983, 1984) have examined the consequences of "staying power," where one player can make his initial strategy choice *after* the other and stay at this outcome until after the other player moves from it, and "threat power" where, in an iterated game, one player can threaten to move to a Pareto-inferior outcome to deter the other player from making undesired choices in *subsequent* games.

not moving (i.e., passing) from an initial outcome,[7] is assumed to be able to stay, move, *or* hold.

More formally, the concept of holding power emends as follows the rules that constitute the initial definition of sequential play within the theory of moves (see chapter 2):

I. Both players simultaneously choose strategies, thereby defining an initial outcome of the game or, alternately, an initial outcome is imposed on the players by empirical circumstances.

II. Once at an initial outcome, the player with holding power can either move to a subsequent outcome or "pass" and force the player without holding power to make the first move.[8] Whatever H decides, NH can respond by either staying (and hence, terminating the game) or by unilaterally switching his strategy and moving to a subsequent outcome.

III. Given that NH has not terminated the game, H can respond (a) by unilaterally switching his strategy, thereby changing the subsequent outcome to a new subsequent outcome; (b) by staying and thereby terminating the game himself; or (c) by holding and forcing NH to make the next move.

IV. Given that H has not terminated the game, NH can respond by unilaterally switching his strategy and inducing still another subsequent outcome, or, by not moving, terminating the game.[9]

7. This assumption is necessary lest H be given the ability to terminate movement in a game before it begins.

8. Thus, unlike the notion of staying power (see above, note 6), in which the more powerful player is assumed to move second, the concept of holding power does not restrict the domain of choices initially available to the player who possesses it.

9. This rule and its sequential relationship to Rule III implies that NH will always have an opportunity to respond to a hold or move choice by H. It is for this reason that only games with an *even* number of moves are considered in the determination of a holding power outcome. To be more specific, I assume that each game

V. These strictly alternating moves, with options for H and NH as outlined in III and IV, respectively, continue until the player with the next move chooses not to switch his strategy. When this happens, the game terminates, and the outcome reached is the final (*holding power*) *outcome* of the game.

There are two additional assumptions associated with the definition of holding power. First, consistent with the theory of moves framework adopted herein, is the assumption of *nonmyopic calculations:* players are assumed to make their decisions to move or not to move from any outcome in full anticipation of how each will respond to the other. And second, is the *inertia principle:* a player will not move from any outcome unless he anticipates a *better* outcome as the final outcome. Among other things, this implies that a player without holding power will not move from a position if he anticipates that H will hold and force him rationally to return to it. Thus, implicit in the inertia principle is an aversion to cycling on the part of both players.[10] Perforce, this assumption induces a unique holding-power outcome from every initial outcome. Consequently, along with the assumptions that define absorbing outcomes and limited-move equilibria, the assumptions that define holding power can be considered a third set of stability criteria that can be used to overcome the indeterminacy problem associated with unilateral deterrence games.

---

terminates after a (sufficiently) large even number of opportunities to move. Since the final outcome implied by this assumption does not depend upon the precise number of moves and countermoves available to the players, the holding power outcome can be interpreted as the outcome that results from a sequence of play by far-sighted, albeit unequally weighted, players.

10. The inertia principle should be contrasted with the termination condition associated with the concept of a nonmyopic equilibrium—discussed in chapter 2—and the assumption of *rational termination* associated with the concept of staying power. Since a player with staying power, S, is assumed to make the second move in a sequential game, he will always be the player in the position to complete the cycle. Rational termination assumes (a) that S will always complete the cycle unless he obtains his best outcome by staying, and (b) that the player without staying power will not move unless he can obtain a better outcome before the cycle is complete.

Before illustrating this concept in the context of the 1948
Berlin crisis and exploring its implications for the stability of
deterrence relationships, I should point out that this conception of power differs in fundamental ways from the definition
of capability offered in chapter 2 and discussed in detail in section 4.1. An opponent's capability is assumed to be a factor in
determining a player's preference order, while the notion of
holding power is not such a factor. Rather, the concept of holding power is best interpreted as a measure of the relative ability
of each player to endure the costs implied by his opponent's
capability. In this sense, the concept of capability is analytically prior to the notion of holding power.

Of course, in those (nuclear) relationships where mutual ex-
tinction is the most likely consequence of a confrontation, this
particular measure of power is clearly extraneous. The notion
of holding power is only relevant in a nuclear context when at
least one of the players believes in the possibility of fighting
(and winning) such a war.

4.3 The Berlin Crisis Revisited

To illustrate this concept, it will be useful to consider once
again the Berlin crisis game of 1948. Recall that toward the
end of June, the Western powers announced a currency reform
for both West Germany and West Berlin as preliminary to the
establishment of a German Federal Republic. At this point, the
Soviets had just two broad choices: they could either accept
the Western plan or, by clamping a blockade around Berlin,
create the game depicted in figure 1.1.

The Soviets' motive in inducing the Berlin crisis game and,
in the process, moving from their next-worst outcome, (4,2),
to their worst outcome, (1,1), was rather transparent. As
George and Smoke (1974, 118) have noted, "the blockade was
Moscow's way of saying to the West, you may set up a separate
West German government or you may continue to exercise
your powers in Berlin, but you cannot do both." Put in a

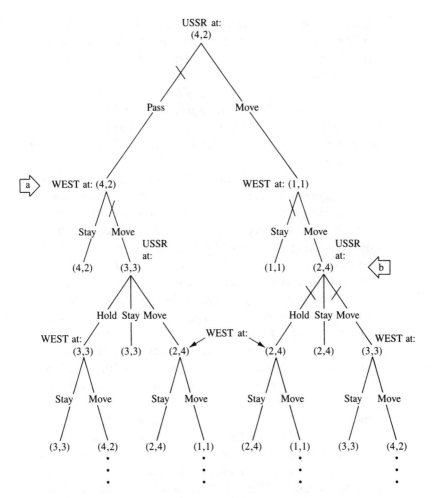

FIGURE 4.4: Game Tree of the Berlin Crisis of 1948, Given That (4,2) Is the Initial Outcome and That the Soviet Union Has Holding Power.

slightly different way, the Soviets believed that they could force
the Western powers to make the next move in the postwar divi-
sion-of-spoils game they were playing with the United States
and its allies.

If, by virtue of the geography of the city of Berlin, the Soviets could compel the West to move, they would have enjoyed
"holding power" in the local theater. As is intuitively clear, the
possession of holding power has only salutary implications for
a player in this game.

For a formal demonstration of this, consider now the game
tree of figure 4.4, which lists the sequence of choices away
from outcome C, (4,2), in the Berlin crisis game. Note that in
contrast to the tree depicted in figure 2.3, which reflects the
initial definition of sequential play in the theory of moves, this
tree reflects rules I to V (see above) associated with the concept of holding power. After a preliminary decision at the initial outcome,[11] the player with holding power is assumed to
have the option of moving, staying, or holding and forcing the
player without holding power to make the next move.

The specification of the holding-power outcome of this
game requires that the implications of each of the two Soviet
choices at the top of the tree be compared. To this end, consider first the sequence of moves on the left side of the tree
which would be induced if the Soviets passed at the initial outcome, (4,2). Although the left side of the tree of figure 4.4
permits an unspecified number of moves and countermoves
away from (4,2), one need not consider the rational choices of
the players past the Western choice at (4,2) in order to discern
the consequences of a Soviet decision to pass at the initial outcome (see the arrow marked "a"). This is because (4,2) represents the best outcome of the Western Alliance. Hence, no
matter what outcome is implied by a Western decision to move
from this outcome, it will never exceed the payoff that the West

11. In the analysis that follows, I consider outcome C, (4,2), to be the pre-
blockade status quo. The subsequent conclusions, however, are robust in the sense that
they do not depend upon this assumption.

can induce by electing to stay there. By the inertia principle, therefore, the rational choice of the West, as indicated by the slash through the move branch leading away from (4,2), is to stay.[12] This means that should the Soviets decide to pass initially, their next-worst outcome is implied as the final outcome of the game.

Similarly, to determine the long-term consequences of a Soviet decision to move away from (4,2), one need consider only the choices prior to the Soviet move at (2,4) on the right side of the tree (see the arrow marked "b"). Since (2,4) represents the best outcome of the Soviet Union, it would not, rationally, hold or move should this outcome be reached in a sequence of moves and countermoves from (4,2).

Given that the rational choice of the Soviets at (2,4) is to stay, what should the West do at the previous node, (1,1)? Clearly, the West will elect to move from its worst outcome to its next-worst outcome (2,4) should the sequential move process reach (1,1). Thus, by moving away from (4,2) initially, and temporarily inducing (1,1), the Soviets can bring about their best outcome (2,4) as the holding-power outcome of this game.

The strategic choice facing the Soviets in late June 1948, then, is summarized by the node at the top of the game tree of figure 4.4. By passing and, in effect, accepting the Western initiative, outcome C, the next-worst outcome of the Soviet Union, is implied. But by moving away from the Nash equilibrium at (4,2) to an ostensively worse outcome at (1,1), the Soviets, because they *believed* that they possessed a tactical advantage, thought that they would force the West to back away from its plan to resurrect West Germany and thereby induce their most-preferred outcome (2,4) as the final outcome of this cold-war game.

Interestingly, a similar, albeit less compelling, explanation of the Soviet decision to blockade Berlin in 1948 can also be

12. Hirshleifer (1985) would call this "natural termination."

constructed without assuming that the Soviets perceived that they possessed holding power. Since (3,3) is the unique non-myopic equilibrium of this game, the Soviets could induce this outcome as the final outcome of the game if an equal distribution of power is postulated. Since the Soviets preferred (3,3) to the initial outcome of this dramatic game of Chicken, i.e., (4,2), their incentive to move from it is established.

Nevertheless, the concept of holding power, and its attribution to the Western powers, *is* required to explain the final resolution of the Berlin crisis game. Without the interpretation that the successful airlift enabled the Western powers to establish their holding power, the long-term (but not the short-term) stability of (4,2), the outcome associated with the eventual Western victory, evaporates. Moreover, only the holding-power model can explain why it was the Soviet Union, and not the Western Alliance, that backed away from the conflictual outcome (1,1).[13] It is precisely for this reason that an explanation of the Berlin crisis game, rooted in the theory of moves and its attendant concepts, is sounder than the analogous explanations—discussed in chapter 1—offered by either an expected utility analysis or classical game-theoretic formulations.

It would be stretching this explanation too far, however, to suggest that Western leaders foresaw that their best outcome would eventually evolve out of this interaction. In fact, the Truman administration was pleasantly surprised by the success of the airlift, but it was shocked by the Soviet move against Berlin that made it necessary (George and Smoke 1974, chap. 5). Thus, had the top decision-makers in the West been a little more prescient, they too might have conceded holding power to the Soviets in Europe and not attempted to circumvent the Potsdam Agreement that established four-power control over Germany.[14]

---

13. I would similarly argue that the holding power implied by the conventional and strategic superiority of the United States in 1962 also explains why the Soviets blinked first in the eyeball-to-eyeball confrontation over the missiles in Cuba.

14. Notice that such a misperception in no way precludes a rational-choice explanation of the decisions made by the players before and after the Berlin crisis game.

4.4 Strategic Implications of Holding Power

In light of the above, it is clear that the ability of a player to exert some control over the sequential move process in a deterrence game may have a dramatic impact on its final resolution. In games like the Berlin crisis of 1948, this ability may permit a player to transcend the liabilities associated with an (inherently) incredible threat, that is, it may render rational, and hence, credible, a decision to stay at, or not move from, an ostensively inferior outcome in order to bring about, ultimately, a better outcome in the long run for the player with holding power.[15]

In general, however, holding power offers a player who possesses it selective benefits.[16] In mutual-deterrence games (see table 4.1), for instance, when both players have a credible threat (Prisoners' Dilemma), the stability of the deterrence relationship is not affected; and when just one player's threat is credible (Called Bluff), that player's victory is still implied.[17] Only in Chicken, when both players lack credibility, will the outcome implied by a balance of power be different than the holding-power outcome. As illustrated above, in Chicken, the more powerful player will win.

As can be seen from table 4.2, the implications of holding power are somewhat different in unilateral-deterrence games. When one player possesses holding power, all four games of unilateral deterrence are rendered determinate. Nevertheless, in three of the four core games, it does not matter which player has it. More specifically, when both players have a credible threat, as in game 64(48), deterrence constitutes a stable relationship as long as either player has holding power. And when only one player has a credible threat, as in games 15(21) and

15. This is the reason for the initial qualification of the concept of credibility given in chapter 2.

16. For the overall impact of holding power in 2 × 2 ordinal games, see Kilgour and Zagare, mimeographed.

17. In another context, Brams (1983) call such games "undecidable." They are undecidable because one cannot infer, just by observing their outcome, whether or not one of the players possesses a power advantage.

TABLE 4.1: Summary of Mutual Deterrence Games Given a Balance and Imbalance of Power

	POWER DISTRIBUTION	
Game	Equal	One player has holding power
Prisoners' Dilemma: both players have a credible threat.	stable deterrence	stable deterrence
Chicken: neither player has a credible threat.	stable deterrence	player with holding power wins
Called Bluff: one player has a credible threat.	player with a credible threat wins	player with a credible threat wins

TABLE 4.2: Summary of Unilateral Deterrence Games Given a Balance and Imbalance of Power

	POWER DISTRIBUTION		
Game	Equal	Status Quo player has holding power	Revisionist player has holding power
64(48): both players have a credible threat.	indeterminate	stable deterrence	stable deterrence
65(55): neither player has a credible threat.	indeterminate	stable deterrence	revisionist player wins
76(72): status-quo player has a credible threat.	indeterminate	stable deterrence	stable deterrence
15(21): revisionist player has a credible threat.	indeterminate	revisionist player wins	revisionist player wins

76(72), the player with a credible threat, not necessarily the player with holding power, is able to induce his best outcome.

As with mutual-deterrence games, however, the impact of a power imbalance is most crucial to the fortunes of the players when both players lack credibility, as in game 65(55). In this case, deterrence stability is maintained when the status-quo player is more powerful. But this stability is upset, and a loss for the status-quo player is implied, when it is the revisionist player with the power advantage.

In both mutual- and unilateral-deterrence games, therefore, holding power is neither a necessary nor a sufficient condition for deterrence stability. In some games, a more powerful player may be unable to deter a weaker opponent. And in other games, holding power may actually be superfluous in stabilizing the status quo.

4.5 Summary and Conclusions

In this chapter the complications introduced into deterrence relationships by both the absence of a capable retaliatory threat and by power asymmetries were discussed. Capability was shown to be a necessary condition for deterrence stability. This means that a revisionist player whose opponent lacks capability is unable to be punished and, hence, cannot be deterred.[18]

By contrast, the existence of a power imbalance has a variable impact on the deterrence relationship. If (holding) power is defined as one player's ability to stay at and absorb the costs at some outcome longer than another player, then an asymmetric distribution of power is neither sufficient or necessary for deterrence instability. Thus, the analysis of holding power is consistent with the power-transition theory of Organski and Kugler (1980)—power imbalances do not imply war—and may shed some light on the conditions necessary for peaceful power transitions. More specifically, when a revisionist player has holding power and the threat of a status-quo player is not credible, conflict is not implied even though deterrence is unstable. Under these conditions, the status-quo player should accede to, rather than resist, an attempt by his opponent to impose a new order. Moreover, to the extent that conditions of

18. If either player in a deterrence game has the ability to preempt the other with a first strike, the capability of the other player is, in effect, eliminated. This is why deterrence is unstable under these conditions.

power parity contribute to misperceptions about the possession of holding power, one would logically expect transition
periods of approximately equal power to be associated with
the outbreak of major conflict. (Organski and Kugler's [1980,
chap. 1] empirical data support this conclusion.) This is precisely why Quester (1982) has listed just this type of pernicious
misperception among the major causes of international war.

Part II

Applying the Model

5

Explaining the
Middle East Crisis
of 1967

I turn now, in Part II of this book, from the task of theory construction to the business of theory application, from the abstract world of game theory to the convoluted world of international politics. The next three chapters illustrate a variety of application methodologies. In chapter 6, I use the model developed in Part I as a *normative* device to evaluate the strategic rationale offered by the Nixon administration for its decision to place American military forces on a world-wide alert during the October, or Yom Kippur, War between Israel and several Arab states in 1973. And in chapter 7, the deterrence model is used as a *descriptive* tool for evaluating a number of alternative explanations for the stability of the strategic relationship of the United States and the Soviet Union since 1945.

By contrast, the application in the present chapter serves somewhat different purposes. First, in examining three games played during the Middle East crisis of 1967—two of which were played by the United States and Israel prior to the Six-Day War, and one game played by the United States and the Soviet Union during the war—I demonstrate how the model can be used to analyze actual international conflicts;[1] and second, this application serves as a basis for assessing the *explan-*

1. Almost any international crisis is made up of several concurrent, overlapping games between various combinations of principal and peripheral actors. Although no attempt is made here to examine all of the games played during this crisis, this should not be interpreted to imply that there were not other significant games played at this time.

atory power of the theory of moves and comparing it with that
of more standard game-theoretic formulations.[2]

5.1 The First United States-Israel Game

The Middle East crisis of 1967 was precipitated by a rapid-
fire series of events that culminated on May 22 when Egyptian
president Gamal Abdel Nasser ordered the Strait of Tiran closed
to Israeli shipping and to strategic cargo bound for Israel. As
early as 1957, Israel had announced that such action would be
considered a *casus belli* (Perlmutter 1978, 21). By closing the
Strait, Nasser was blocking Israel's only outlet to the Indian
Ocean and had reversed the one tangible gain made by Israel in
the 1956 war. After that war, Israel had agreed to withdraw
from occupied territory in return for a United States assurance
that it considered the Gulf of Aqaba an international waterway,
and for supervision of the Strait by the United Nations. Thus,
after Nasser ordered the United Nations Emergency Force
(UNEF) from the Gaza Strip and Sharm al-Shaykh (May 17),
and then declared the Strait closed, Israeli foreign minister
Abba Eban told French president Charles de Gaulle that Israel
had just two options:

1. Submit to Nasser's attempted fait accompli, or
2. Resist Egypt by using force to reopen the Strait.

It was clear to all that the choice of the second option would
trigger Israel's third war with neighboring Arab states.

For reasons to be given shortly, it was the preference of the
United States, Israel's protector, to prevent war that linked the
two countries in games to be examined presently. United States
decision-makers, like Israel's, seriously considered two strategies during this game:

2. The rest of this chapter is based upon Frank C. Zagare, "Nonmyopic Equilibria
and the Middle East Crisis of 1967," *Conflict Management and Peace Science* 5
(Spring 1981), and is used with the permission of the editors of that journal.

1. Withhold full political and military support of Israel's demand that the Strait be opened immediately, or

2. Back Israel by either taking or supporting action designed to reopen the Strait.

The Possible Outcomes of the First Game

Given the options of Israel and the United States at the time that Nasser closed the Strait, four outcomes of this alliance game seemed possible (see figure 5.1):

A. *The Status Quo of May 22.* If the United States withheld full support of Israel's demands, and Israel submitted to Nasser's actions by refraining from a military response, the Strait of Tiran would remain closed to Israeli shipping, pending a possible diplomatic initiative in the United Nations, or a multilateral naval force organized by the United States (dubbed the Red Sea Regatta by undersecretary of state Eugene Rostow) that would patrol the Strait and guarantee Israel access to the Gulf of Aqaba.[3] United States decision-makers did not think that the latter action would provoke a Soviet response (Safran 1969, 310).

B. *United States Opens Strait.* Unilateral American action on behalf of Israel was also thought unlikely to precipitate war in the region (Dayan 1976, 320). Like a multilateral initiative, a unilateral American solution would also force the Strait open, and would not necessarily affirm Israel's "right" of passage. In addition, this outcome opened the United States to possible political or economic retaliation from the Arab states.

---

3. There was, of course, no guarantee that such United States-backed efforts would succeed in reopening the Strait. As will be seen, Israel's preference regarding this outcome depended upon its evaluation of the future consequences associated with it.

If Israel resisted Nasser's move by using military force to reopen the Strait, this action would precipitate a third Arab-Israeli war and immediately raise the probability of a super-power confrontation leading, possibly, to World War III. United States decisions in this case would produce the following likely outcomes:

> C. *Israel Isolated.* If the United States withheld support of an Israeli military action designed to return the Middle East to the status quo ante, Israel would still most likely win a short war with its Arab neighbors and reopen the Strait. However, if the war remained local, and a super-power confrontation were avoided, Israel would find itself isolated diplomatically and thus subject to heavy political pressure, especially from the United States, to withdraw from any territory it might occupy.

		ISRAEL	
		Submit	**Resist**
UNITED STATES	**Withhold Full Support**	A. US–USSR confrontation avoided; US seeks diplomatic solution in UN or organizes multilateral naval force; Strait remains closed and Israel mobilizes.	C. Possible US–USSR confrontation; Arab-Israeli war; Strait opened; Israel isolated diplomatically.
	Back Israel	B. US–USSR confrontation avoided; US unilaterally opens Strait thereby alienating the Arab states.	D. Possible US–USSR confrontation; Arab–Israeli war; Strait opened; Israel supported by US; US alienates Arab states.

FIGURE 5.1: Outcome Matrix of the First United States–Israel Game

D. *Israel Supported*. If the United States supported Israel's military action, Israel would be in a better position to consolidate its gains after the war. But from the American point of view, support of Israel, as before (Outcome B), ran the risk of alienating the oil-producing Arab states and, as Nasser had threatened, losing access to the Suez Canal (Bar-Zohar 1970, 141).

American and Israeli Preferences

American preferences throughout this crisis were relatively straightforward. More than anything, United States decision-makers wanted to avoid an Arab-Israeli war that could, willy-nilly, involve both the United States and the Soviet Union in a major confrontation. Indeed, even before Nasser had closed the Strait, United States president Lyndon Johnson (1971, 290) decided to throw "the full weight of U.S. diplomacy into an effort to forestall war." Thus, the first preference of the American government was the status quo of May 22, outcome A.

How would the United States respond, however, if war did break out in the region? For reasons to be discussed shortly, United States decision-makers were not completely honest when this question was posed by Israeli leaders at several points during this crisis. As will be seen, there were important reasons for the United States to lead Israel to believe that it would *not* support an Israeli military action to reopen Aqaba— that is, that it preferred outcome C to outcome D. However, because President Johnson wanted to honor previous United States commitments, and because he felt that "Israel had a right to that access to the sea," the United States position was decidedly in favor of supporting Israel politically and, if necessary, militarily. As Johnson (1971, 295) later remarked, "if it came to a crunch, I believed the American flag would have to sail the waters of Aqaba alongside Israel's." Consequently, while its apparent preference was for outcome D over outcome

C, the announced preference of the United States was for C over D.

Finally, the United States least preferred to take unilateral military action to reopen the Strait, outcome B. Because of its deep involvement in Vietnam at this time, the United States feared overextending itself with another military operation in a situation that did not seem to require that it act alone (Quandt 1977, 40; Bar-Zohar 1970, 84). In addition, there was little political support in the Senate for unilateral action in the Middle East (Johnson 1971, 292).

Until the end of May, however, the Israeli leadership believed that if the various diplomatic options (outcome A) fell through, the United States was prepared to act alone (outcome B). It is not clear whether Israel's interpretation of the United States position on unilateral action was a deliberate (self?) deception, or simply a misunderstanding (see below). At any rate, although the United States preference order was (A,D,C,B), Israeli decision-makers perceived it to be (A,B,C,D).

In contrast to the preferences of the United States, Israel's were more complex, for they fluctuated over time. Nevertheless, throughout this crisis, Israel's main objective was to reopen the Strait and to reverse the psychological victory Nasser had achieved by closing it. Since, initially, all four outcomes seemed to offer some possibility of reopening the Strait, Israel's preferences hinged upon the benefits, weighed against the concomitant costs, of each of the four possible outcomes.

To reopen the Strait, Israel most preferred to take military action and demonstrate to the Arab nations that continuing belligerency involved significant costs. Still, Israel's enthusiasm for the military option was dulled by the realization that American diplomatic help was necessary to translate a military triumph into a meaningful political victory. Accordingly, Israel's first preference was to force the reopening of the Strait, given the backing and support of the United States government (i.e., outcome D).

Despite its own, and American, intelligence estimates that it would easily win a war with some, or all, of the Arab states (Khouri 1968, 258), Israel initially preferred to give others a chance (outcomes A and B) to return the region to the status quo ante, rather than risk political and military isolation at outcome C (Bar-Zohar 1970, 135). Moreover, I assume that Israeli leaders favored a multilateral solution (outcome A), which would demonstrate broad-based support of its position, to a unilateral American initiative (outcome B), which might suggest Israeli impotence and dependence on the United States for its defense and survival.[4] Thus, during the first days of this crisis, Israel's preference order was (D,A,B,C).

As will be seen, however, after May 28, when it became apparent that there was little possibility of multilateral action, Israel's preference-order shifted. At this point, Israel's decision-makers came to prefer all other outcomes, including unilateral military action, to accepting the status quo. Thus, Israel's preference order became (D,B,C,A). In the next section, I will demonstrate that this shift in Israel's preferences, together with a reevaluation of United States intentions, had important consequences for the manner in which this crisis was resolved.

A Theory-of-Moves Analysis

To understand the behavior of the United States and Israel during the first stage of this crisis, it will be useful to examine the dynamics of two distinct games: the first, based on Israel's mistaken perception of American preferences, is the game that was actually played; the second is the game that would have been played had Israel correctly construed the preferences of the United States. The payoff matrices for these two games are depicted in figures 5.2 and 5.4 respectively.

Before proceeding, I should point out a salient empirical

4. This assumption is not necessary for the subsequent analysis.

ISRAEL

		Submit	Resist
UNITED STATES	**Withhold Full Support**	A. STATUS QUO (4,3)	C. ISRAEL ISOLATED (2,1)
	Back Israel	B. U.S. OPENS STRAIT (3,2)	D. ISRAEL SUPPORTED (1,4)

FIGURE 5.2: Payoff Matrix of the First United States–Israel Game, Given Israel's Perception of American Preferences

constraint that limited the ability of the players to make *all* of the logically possible moves and countermoves in each of these games. More specifically, movement back from either outcome C to outcome A, or from D to B, was not likely. Generally, it is not possible for a state in an alliance game suddenly to reverse its strategy after precipitating a war. Under such circumstances, the termination of hostilities also depends upon the preferences and strategy choices of the state(s) being attacked (Wittman 1979). In this particular case, it is clear that, once Israel selected its resist strategy, it could not suddenly switch back to its submit strategy, although the United States could, if it preferred, respond after an Israeli resist decision. This means that, given an Israeli move from the status quo of May 22, outcome A, a total of only two moves—one by Israel and one by the United States—was possible. Hence, in gauging the long-term stability of this outcome (i.e., A) in the subsequent discussion, I will use the concept of a Type II limited-move equilibrium (see chapter 2).

Why did Israel refrain from taking military steps to reopen the Strait during the period covered by the first game? The

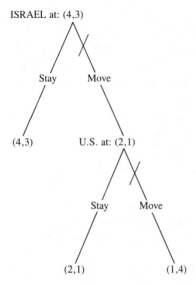

ISRAEL at: (4,3)

Stay   Move

(4,3)   U.S. at: (2,1)

Stay   Move

(2,1)   (1,4)

FIGURE 5.3: Game Tree of the First United States–Israel Game, Starting with Israel at (4,3)

brief answer to this question is that outcome A was stable in the long-term sense of a Type II limited-move equilibrium, that is, Israel could not induce a better outcome by unilaterally switching to a strategy that did not support the status quo of May 22.

To see this, consider now the game tree of figure 5.3 which depicts the sequence of *empirically* possible moves and countermoves away from the status quo by the United States and Israel in this game.[5] Since it is Israel's behavior that is to be explained here, the preferences used in Figure 5.3 to calculate the long-term consequences of an Israeli strategy switch are the postulated preferences of Israel (for this period) and its *perception* of United States preferences.

5. Note the truncated tree required to determine whether or not an outcome is a Type II equilibrium.

As before, Israel's incentive to switch or not to switch from its status-quo strategy (outcome A) can be determined by simply working backwards up the tree and asking what the rational choice for each player would be at each node or decision point. At the last node of this tree, the United States must decide whether to stay at (2,1) and withhold support of Israel—its next-worst outcome—or back Israel by moving to (1,4)—its worst outcome—which would become the final outcome of the game. Clearly, given its perception of American preferences, the Israeli leadership would expect the United States to stay at (2,1).

In light of the expected American choice at (2,1), should Israel depart from its status-quo strategy? Since the sequence of moves would terminate at (2,1)—Israel's worst outcome—if it departs, and the status quo is its postulated next-best outcome, it is plainly not advantageous for Israel to change its strategy. Thus, the status quo, (4,3), is stable in the long-term sense *for Israel*.

This outcome is also stable in the long-term sense *for the United States*. Since the status quo is its best outcome, a similar analysis of the consequences of an initial departure from the status quo by the United States would obviously reveal that there is no incentive for the United States to switch from its withhold-support strategy associated with the status quo.

The lack of incentive on the part of *both* players to depart from this outcome renders the status quo a Type II limited-move equilibrium. It is precisely the long-term stability of this outcome that provides an explanation of Israel's decision not to pursue military options to reopen the Strait during the first game of this crisis.

Why did the United States mislead Israel about its preference for outcome D over C? Simply because a truthful American announcement would have destroyed the dynamic stability of the status quo, the best outcome of the United States. To see this, consider for a moment the payoff matrix of figure 5.4,

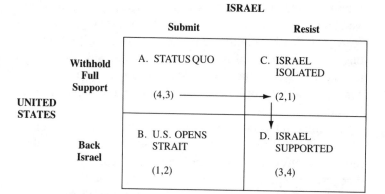

FIGURE 5.4: Payoff Matrix of the First United States–Israel Game, Given a Correct Israeli Assessment of American Preferences

which gives the postulated true American preferences.[6] As noted above, it is this game that would have been played if the United States had been completely honest about its preferences, or if Israeli intelligence had been able to detect the American deception. It is easy to see that the status quo is not stable in the long-term sense in this game.

Israel's incentive to depart from the status quo can be seen by following the path of the arrows in figure 5.4. If Israel switched from (4,3) to (2,1), the United States would rationally move from (2,1) to (3,4). Since Israel prefers (3,4) to the status quo (4,3), it would have had an incentive in this game to change strategies; and since the United States preferred (4,3) to (3,4), it had an incentive to misrepresent its preferences in order to remove Israel's incentive to precipitate war.[7]

It is important to point out that (4,3) is also a Nash equilibrium in the game of figure 5.2, and thus also explains the

6. This matrix assumes that Israel was also completely informed about the preference of the United States for outcome B. The following analysis does not rest upon this assumption.

7. For a game-theoretic analysis of the strategy of deception in two-person games, see Brams (1977), and in three-person games Brams and Zagare (1977, 1981).

stability of the status quo in the game actually played. However, since (4,3), as well as (3,4), is also a Nash equilibrium in figure 5.4, Nash's equilibrium concept does not pick up the long-term *instability* of the status quo in the game that would have been played if the United States had not deceived Israel. Hence, it fails to provide an explanation for the American deception.

This interpretation of the motivations underlying the behavior of the United States and Israel is consistent with both their verbal and physical actions during the first game of the May-June crisis. Throughout this game, the United States persistently sought a diplomatic escape, first by attempting to organize a multilateral naval force to guarantee Israel's access to Aqaba, then by exploring various options in the United Nations, and finally by seeking a compromise with Nasser. At the same time, key United States decision-makers tried to restrain Israel by warning, continuously, that diplomatic and, if necessary, military support would be withheld if Israel initiated a war. Conversely, the Israeli diplomatic effort was directed at inducing the United States to make a public commitment (or at least give private assurances) that it would guarantee Israel's sovereignty if it were threatened. However, as long as the Israeli preference order remained as postulated, Israel's actions were circumspect.

As already noted, the United States effort to restrain Israel began even before Nasser closed Aqaba. On May 17, one day after UNEF was ordered from Egyptian territory, President Johnson (1971, 290) cabled Israeli Prime Minister Levi Eshkol and warned that he could not "accept any responsibilities on behalf of the United States which arise as the result of actions on which we are not consulted." Three days later (May 20), the president's message was underscored, albeit in more colorful language, by Eugene Rostow in a meeting with two Israeli diplomats. "If you want us to be with you at the crash landing," Rostow warned, "then you had better consult us at the takeoff" (Bar-Zohar 1970, 56).

The closing of the Strait on May 22 merely heightened an already tense situation. To prevent a spasm attack, the United States asked the Israelis to delay taking action for forty-eight hours. Because the Israeli leadership wanted United States support and, in addition, did not want to alienate Johnson, they acceded to the American appeal. Some Israeli politicians, however, interpreted the request for delay to imply that Israel would have an American carte blanche after a two-day wait. Others argued that Israel should go to war at that time regardless of the position of the United States. All the while, Israel's general mobilization was moving toward completion (Bar-Zohar 1970, 76–84).

Given this sentiment of the Israeli leadership, it is not surprising that they were dismayed with the United States proposal (on May 25) to organize a multilateral naval force to reopen the Strait and patrol the Gulf. Rather than acquiesce to the American plan, they decided to force the issue by instructing foreign minister Abba Eban to inform Johnson that an Egyptian surprise attack was imminent. When Johnson was told of this, he immediately contacted both the Egyptians and their Soviet sponsors to urge their restraint, though his message to them fell short of the Israeli request that he state that he would regard an attack against Israel as an attack on the United States (Bar-Zohar 1970, 106–11).

The following day, Eban pressed for a meeting with Johnson, claiming that he had to return to Israel that night for a decisive cabinet meeting. In the interim, three separate American intelligence groups reported to the president that an Egyptian attack was *not* about to take place. Correctly sensing that Eban was trying to pressure him into a quick decision, Johnson reportedly exploded, telling one aide, "I don't like anyone to put a pistol to my head. This Sunday cabinet meeting of his to decide on peace or war—it's an ultimatum, and I don't like it" (Bar-Zohar 1970, 116). Nevertheless, Johnson did meet with Eban, Israeli Ambassador Avraham Harmon, and others at 7:00 P.M. on May 26.

There is some question about exactly what Johnson said at this meeting. In his memoirs, Johnson (1971, 294) claimed that he said he "would, within the limits of [his] constitutional position, be making a maximum effort" to reopen the Strait. On the other hand, Harmon's record of the minutes of this meeting quoted Johnson as saying that he would "use any or all measures to open the Straits" (Brecher 1975, 392).[8] All accounts agree, however, that Johnson repeated, in a slow, deliberate manner, a phrase that echoed his previous warning. At least twice Johnson (1971, 293) emphasized that Israel would "not be alone unless it decides to go alone."

On May 27, Eban returned to Israel to take part in the pending cabinet debate. At this meeting, Eban outlined Johnson's request that Israel wait for two or three weeks to allow him time to pursue a diplomatic solution, and repeated Johnson's warning about the consequences of unilateral action. He also reported his version of Johnson's pledge to take "any and all measures" to return the area to the status quo ante. Although it would be difficult to posit a direct causal relationship, it is likely that Eban's account of his meeting with Johnson was not without impact on the nine-to-nine deadlock that night in the cabinet on a motion to declare war.

After this vote, the cabinet meeting was adjourned until the next day. But before the cabinet could reconvene, the Israeli leadership was inundated with messages—a cable from Johnson, a dispatch from Secretary of State Dean Rusk, a note from de Gaulle, and a letter from British prime minister Harold Wilson—all urging Israel not to attack Egypt. Later Eshkol claimed that it was the communications from Johnson and Rusk, which reiterated the warning about Israel's potential isolation, that were instrumental in the nearly unanimous decision of the cabinet on May 28 to delay going to war (Brecher 1975, 401).

---

8. As will be seen, this misunderstanding was clarified during the second phase of this crisis.

5.2 The Second United States–Israel Game

The first game of this crisis began to unravel shortly after the May 28 cabinet meeting. The immediate precipitant of the process that would generate a second game by June 4 was the signing of a mutual defense pact by Egypt and Jordan on May 30. Because Israel was especially vulnerable to attack from the Jordanian border, the Israeli cabinet decided to reconsider the rationale for further delay. As will be seen, the reevaluation process was noteworthy because it produced a new consensus on the bankruptcy of President Johnson's plan to reopen Aqaba by organizing a multilateral naval force, and because it resulted in general agreement that the United States was unwilling to take unilateral action to return the region to the status quo ante.

As the reevaluation process began, the cabinet received a cable from Ambassador Harmon reporting his opinion that little international support existed for coordinated naval action to guarantee Israel access to Aqaba (Brecher 1974, 412–13). The possibility that the United States plan might fall through prompted Prime Minister Eshkol to write to Johnson to seek reconfirmation of Eban's interpretation of the United States position of May 26. In this letter, Eshkol pointed out that it was "crucial that the international naval escort should move through the Strait within a week or two" (Johnson 1971, 294), adding that he was pleased by Johnson's assurance that the United States would take "any and all measures to open the Straits of Tiran to international shipping" (Brecher 1975, 414).

Johnson reacted with predictable displeasure to Eshkol's note. On his orders, presidential assistant Walt Rostow phoned Israeli Minister Ephraim Evron to deny that Johnson had guaranteed unilateral action. Later that day, as if to underscore Johnson's message, Secretary of State Rusk told a congressional committee that the United States was "not contemplating any unilateral move in the Middle East" (Bar-Zohar 1970, 161).

Meanwhile, evidence began to accumulate that reinforced

Harmon's evaluation of the likelihood of a multilateral initiative. Just prior to Rusk's comments, Harmon himself was sounded out by the Rostow brothers about his reaction to a possible bargain with Nasser (Bar-Zohar 1970, 160–61). Moreover, "rumors began to circulate in Washington on May 31 that the United States was looking for possible compromises to end the crisis" (Quandt 1977, 57). Finally, Meir Amit, the head of Israeli intelligence who was in Washington to confer with Defense Department officials, reported to the cabinet that "the maritime force project is running into heavier water every hour" (Brecher 1975, 417).

Given the apparent unwillingness of the United States to act alone, and the high probability that multilateral action would not materialize, opinion in the Israeli cabinet began to shift to the conviction that further delay was counterproductive. This was evidenced by political pressures that forced Prime Minister Eshkol to resign his other post of defense minister and offer it to Moshe Dayan, a hard-liner who was known to favor Israeli military action. Even Abba Eban, a leading proponent of caution, confessed to some cabinet members on June 1 that he saw no good reason to delay using force (Brecher 1975, 417).

On June 3, President Johnson's official response to Eshkol's (May 30) cable arrived in Israel. In the letter, Johnson repeated, again, his warning that Israel would be isolated if it acted without consultation. Furthermore, he was straightforward in revealing the limits of the United States position. "Our leadership is unanimous," he wrote, "that the United States should not move in isolation" (Brecher 1975, 420).

Thus, when the Israeli cabinet met again on June 4, its perception of the American position, as well as its evaluation of the status quo, outcome A, was quite different from what it had been on May 28. Now the Israeli leadership recognized that the United States was averse to acting alone. In addition, because they came to believe that continued pursuit of a diplomatic solution would most likely result in concessions to Nasser, they came to prefer all other outcomes, including taking military action and risking diplomatic isolation, to the status quo of May 22. As of June 4, then, the Israeli preference order was (D,B,C,A).[9]

It is difficult to say whether a majority of the cabinet expected American support for military action by June 4, although there is some evidence that suggests that several top Israeli decision-makers, including Eban and Amit, were convinced that Johnson would not abandon Israel (Quandt 1977, 56; Brecher 1975, 417, 420–21). Whatever the case, Israel's behavior in the second game can be explained without reference to its perception of the American position on this point. But because the actions of the United States after June 4 did depend on its preference to support Israel, it will be assumed that the Israeli leadership expected American assistance if necessary.

To illustrate the consequences of the new Israeli preference order, consider now the payoff matrix of the second United States–Israel game depicted in figure 5.5. Given the new Israeli preferences, it is clear that the status quo is no longer a Type II equilibrium, for this outcome was now Israel's worst. Moreover, Israel could induce a more preferred outcome by switching from submission to resistance, regardless of the response of the United States. But given the preferences of the United States, American support of an Israeli military action was to be expected, should Israel switch to a strategy of resistance. (See the arrows in figure 5.5.)

Not surprisingly, then, on June 4 the Israeli cabinet voted to go to war. The following day, the Israeli air force attacked Egypt. Because Israel quickly gained the upper hand in the en-

9. If the Israelis had continued to perceive a United States willingness to take unilateral action when its multilateral effort fell through (i.e., that the United States preferred outcome B to outcome A), one of six other possible games would have been induced by this alteration of the Israeli preference order. Space considerations preclude a discussion of these six games, though in each of these, the status quo would *not* have been either a nonmyopic or a Nash equilibrium. The point here, however, is that the new Israeli perception of the United States preference order, in conjunction with the shift in its own preference order, is significant because it induced the game depicted in figure 5.5 (see below) rather than one of these six other games.

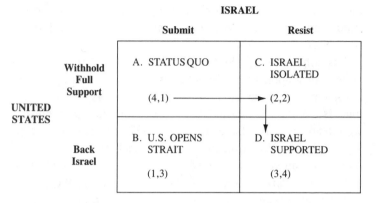

FIGURE 5.5: Payoff Matrix of the Second United States–Israel Game

suing conflict, American support at the local level was not necessary. However, as will be seen in the next section, the United States did *not* abandon Israel after the war, as it had in 1956, by pressing Israel to withdraw from Arab territory. And more significantly, although the United States did attempt to set bounds on the extent of the Israeli victory, it worked to preclude Soviet intervention on behalf of Egypt and Syria.

5.3 The Superpower Game

The outbreak of war on June 5 precipitated the game that President Johnson had long tried to avoid. This game, though, did not involve the United States with Israel, but rather pitted the United States against the Soviet Union. What entangled the two superpowers in this game was the very real possibility that the territorial integrity and independence of Egypt or Syria—allies of the Soviet Union—or less likely, of Israel, might be jeopardized. In such a situation, the superpower whose client was being threatened would be faced with a choice of intervening to prevent the collapse of its ally and to protect its interests in the region, or to remain uninvolved. The other superpower, by contrast, would have to decide whether to restrain its ally or support its impending victory.

President Johnson's apprehension of this game can be appreciated by examining the consequences implied by these options, and the preferences of the superpowers regarding them. Since the Israeli attack on June 5 virtually destroyed the Egyptian and Syrian air forces, it was the Soviet Union that had to decide whether to intervene, while the United States was confronted with the choice of curbing or encouraging Israel. The subsequent analysis takes this empirical reality as its starting point. Of course, had the Arab states achieved military dominance, the roles and the strategies of the superpowers would have been reversed.

The possible outcomes of the superpower game are summarized in figure 5.6. In bilateral terms, a smashing defeat of the Arabs by Israel would result in an American victory over the Soviet Union in a key arena of their wider global competition (Bar-Zohar 1970, 220). Similarly, unilateral Soviet intervention, if only to defend Egypt or Syria, would enable the Soviets to score an important psychological victory and to be in a

| | SOVIET UNION | |
	Not Intervene	Intervene
Restrain Israel	A. COMPROMISE. Limited Israeli victory. (3,3)	C. SOVIET VICTORY. Soviet influence in Middle East enhanced. (1,4)
Encourage Israel	B. U.S. VICTORY. Soviet influence diminished. (4,1)	D. NUCLEAR CONFRONTATION. (2,2)

UNITED STATES

FIGURE 5.6: **Outcome Matrix for the 1967 Superpower Game**

strong position to play a dominant role in determining the political structure of the region after the war.

On the other hand, a compromise of sorts might be worked out if the two superpowers reached a modus vivendi about the limits of the Arab defeat.[10] And finally, if both superpowers intervened—the Soviets to help Egypt and Syria, the United States to counter the Soviet move—the probability of a superpower confrontation, most likely leading to a nuclear clash, would be very high.

In this game, it is clear that, ceteris paribus, both the United States and the Soviet Union most preferred the outcome that maximized the influence of Israel and the pro-Soviet regimes in Egypt and Syria, respectively, and failing that, the compromise outcome.[11] The key question about the preferences of the two superpowers, therefore, is whether or not each would have risked a nuclear confrontation to prevent the spread of the other's influence in the region.

Previously, the preference of the United States to support Israel was discussed. Notwithstanding the sentiments of some Arabists in the State Department, the sympathies of key United States decision-makers, especially President Johnson, were with Israel. This will be demonstrated in a moment. Moreover, all signs indicate that the Soviet Union was similarly committed to its own client states. On May 26, for instance, President Johnson received a cable from Soviet premier Alexei Kosygin warning that "if Israel begins hostilities, the Soviet Union will come to the aid of the attacked countries" (Bar-Zohar 1970, 130). United States decision-makers certainly labored under the assumption that the Soviet Union was prepared to intervene, if intervention became necessary (e.g., Johnson 1971, 302). And early in the crisis, at least, dispatches from American diplomats in Cairo reported that Arab leaders expected Soviet support (Bar-Zohar 1970, 48).

10. Of course, Israeli self-restraint would eliminate the need for positive United States action.
11. As will be seen in chapter 6, this level of American support for Israel would erode by 1973.

Although it is possible that one or both of the superpowers was bluffing, there is no good reason to believe this to be the case. So, whatever the truth of the matter, the reality of June 1967 rested upon the perception of the leaders of both states that the other was willing to run the risk of nuclear war.

Given this reality, the game played by the superpowers at this time was Prisoners' Dilemma. There are, of course, two nonmyopic equilibria in this game. Fortunately for the United States and the Soviet Union, the compromise outcome, (3,3), which constituted the status quo on June 5, was one of them. Since neither player could, in the long run, induce a better outcome than the status quo by departing from it, deterrence constituted a stable relationship during the crisis of 1967.

The second nonmyopic equilibrium is (2,2). Had this outcome been the initial outcome of the 1967 superpower crisis, neither player would have had an incentive to change to another strategy because the superpower with the next move would immediately terminate the sequential move process at the outcome best for it—either (4,1) or (1,4)—and worst for the departing state.

More significant, however, is the fact that (2,2) is an attractive equilibrium while (3,3) is not. As pointed out previously, this means that rational movement from any outcome in this game other than (3,3) leads rationally to (2,2) rather than to (3,3).[12] Thus, the balance of terror in Prisoners' Dilemma is indeed delicate, and President Johnson's apprehension about playing such a game with the Soviets in 1967 is more than understandable. The danger of the war getting out of hand, of an unforeseen incident, or of mutual misperception, might cause a temporary oscillation from the status quo that could involve the superpowers in a nuclear confrontation that both wished to avoid.

The fragile nature of this deterrence equilibrium also explains the behavior of both superpowers during the Six-Day

12. Absorbing outcomes—discussed in chapter 3—are attractive in the same sense.

War.[13] As will be seen, throughout this phase of the crisis, each superpower attempted to bring the local war to a quick end, and—to prevent the other's intervention—displayed a resolve to protect its vital interests in the region. Because of the structure of this game, such behavior was both necessary and sufficient for maintaining the stability of the compromise outcome.

On June 5, almost as soon as United States decision-makers learned of Israel's attack, Secretary of State Rusk, acting on Johnson's orders, cabled Moscow and informed the Soviets that the United States was willing to cooperate to bring "this fighting to an end as quickly as possible" (Johnson 1971, 297). At the same time, United States diplomats in the United Nations were instructed to pursue an immediate cease-fire.

The initial Soviet reaction to the war was also measured. Premier Kosygin contacted Johnson over the "hot line," the first time this communication channel had been officially activated. Kosygin told Johnson that the Soviet Union would intervene if the United States supported Israel. The contingent nature of this threat, however, indicated that the Soviets were not yet prepared to become directly involved in the local conflict (Bar-Zohar 1970, 213).

All of this suddenly changed later in the day. By the afternoon, Israel had attacked Syria, Jordan, and Iraq, and news of the destruction of the Egyptian air force had reached Moscow. Again, Kosygin used the hot line but this time he warned Johnson that the Soviets would act to end the war if Israel did not stop fighting and withdraw to the 1956 armistice lines. Johnson quickly responded, first by calling Kosygin to remind the Soviets of the American commitment to Israel, and second, by ordering the Sixth Fleet to move toward the fighting zone (Bar-Zohar 1970, 218–19). Then, rather than intervene, the Soviets decided to break diplomatic relations with Israel and began to push for a cease-fire in the United Nations. But

13. Given the potential dangers associated with the confrontation outcome in this game, one would expect each superpower to attempt to preempt the other if this game were Chicken, or if either superpower thought it was Chicken.

because Israel and the United States favored a cease-fire in place, while the Arab states and the Soviet Union insisted on a cease-fire that would restore the status quo ante, the fighting continued.

By the next day (June 6), Israeli troops had captured the Gaza Strip and were advancing into Egypt and Jordan. To protect their clients from further defeat, and to eliminate the possibility that the war might get out of hand, the Soviets suddenly reversed their previous position and announced that they would support an unconditional cease-fire. Later that night, however, the Arab states rejected a Security Council resolution calling for an immediate end to the fighting (Khouri 1968, 264).

June 7 saw a further deterioration of the Arab position. The Arab part of Jerusalem fell, Sharm al-Shaykh was captured, and the Mitla Pass taken, cutting off Egyptian troops from retreat to the Suez Canal. Again, Kosygin used the hot line to urge Johnson to restrain Israel (Bar-Zohar 1970, 238), and again, the Egyptians rejected a Security Council resolution calling for a cease-fire (Khouri 1968, 264), although after the West Bank was overrun, the Jordanian government accepted a truce. That night, Defense Minister Dayan announced that Israel had "attained its political and military objectives" (Bar-Zohar 1970, 240).

On the fourth day of the war, a bizarre incident almost triggered World War III. Early on June 8, Israeli war planes attacked an unmarked American intelligence ship, the *Liberty,* killing ten and wounding over one hundred. Reasoning that the Soviets were probably responsible, Johnson quickly put the Strategic Air Command on alert, while nearby American carrier aircraft rushed to the *Liberty* to offer aid and to investigate. It is very likely that the Soviet leadership was unnerved when they were told of this sudden movement of several dozen American planes. Fortunately, an Israeli cable explaining the incident, and a hasty explanation to the Soviets over the hot line, averted disaster (Johnson 1971, 300–301).

By the end of the day, however, Israel had captured the entire Sinai Peninsula and Egypt joined Jordan in accepting a cease-fire. Now, only Syria, a nation that President Johnson (1971, 310) described as the Soviet Union's "special protégé," was still fighting.

Within two days, Israel had moved deep into Syria and was in a position to threaten Damascus. Once more, Kosygin used the hot line. "Kosygin said a 'very crucial moment' had now arrived. He spoke of the possibility of 'independent action' by Moscow. He foresaw the risk of a 'grave catastrophe' and stated that unless Israel unconditionally halted operations within the next few hours, the Soviet Union would take 'necessary actions, including military'" (Johnson 1971, 302).

Johnson's reaction to this message is particularly revealing. First, he ordered the Sixth Fleet to change course and head toward the Syrian coast. As Johnson (1971, 302) noted, this action showed "that the United States was prepared to resist Soviet intrusion in the Middle East." Second, the Israelis were told that they had to stop their advance immediately (Bar-Zohar 1970, 260). Finally, Johnson informed Kosygin that he "had been pressing Israel to make the cease-fire completely effective and had received assurances that this would be done" (Johnson 1971, 303). Soon afterward, Israel announced to the Security Council that a cease-fire had been arranged. The war was over and a superpower confrontation avoided.

5.4 Summary and Conclusions

In this chapter I have applied the theory of moves and its attendant equilibrium concepts to three games played during the Middle East crisis of 1967. I argue that this framework, which takes into account the long-term consequences of departing from an initial outcome, provides a more satisfying theoretical foundation for empirical application than other, more standard approaches to nonzero-sum games.

Perhaps the most appealing theoretical characteristic of this approach is that it introduces a dynamic element into heretofore static game-theoretic analyses. Moreover, it is based on assumptions that either closely match, or are easily adapted to, the actuality of ongoing, real-life games. As has been seen, the equilibrium concepts associated with the theory of moves are readily calculable and interpretable; and, since this approach is based only on ordinal utilities, it requires fewer heroic assumptions than other decision-theoretic models that rest upon the notion of cardinal utility.[14]

The application of this framework to the 1967 crisis provides an explanation of:

1. the persistence of the status quo, and the rationale for the American deception in the first United States–Israel game;

2. the instability of the status quo, and the dynamic interaction leading to the eventual outcome in the second United States–Israel game; and

3. the durability of the compromise outcome in the superpower game.

By contrast, the explanations offered for these same events by other approaches to nonzero-sum games is less compelling. For instance, while Nash's equilibrium concept coincides with the unique Type II equilibrium in both games played by the United States and Israel—and hence singles out the same outcome as the solution to *these* games (see figures 5.2 and 5.5)— it does not provide an explanation of either the stability of the compromise outcome in the superpower game (see figure 5.6) or for the American deception in the first United States–Israel game which contains two Nash equilibria (see figure 5.4).

In the superpower game, the compromise is stable in the

14. For an example of an expected utility model applied to the 1967 crisis, see Wagner (1974).

long-term sense, but it is not a Nash equilibrium.[15] And in the deception game, since the status quo remains a Nash (but not a Type II) equilibrium given the misrepresentation of preferences by the United States, Nash's equilibrium concept cannot explain the motivation for the American deception.

To be sure, these descriptive deficiencies of Nash's equilibrium concept can be mitigated by introducing additional assumptions that extend the analysis. For example, one could explain the American deception by viewing the first United States–Israel game as a sequential game in which Israel had the first move.[16] Since the outcome that Israel would rationally induce in a sequential game in which it was aware of the true American preferences was worse for the United States than the outcome that Israel did induce given the American deception, one could argue that the United States misrepresented its preferences to avoid an inferior outcome. Similarly, Howard's (1971) theory of metagames could be invoked to explain the stability of the compromise outcome in the superpower game. Since the compromise outcome in the Prisoners' Dilemma metagame is a Pareto-optimal Nash equilibrium and, in addition, the product of a dominant metastrategy of one player and an undominated metastrategy of the other, one could argue that neither the United States nor the Soviet Union departed from the compromise outcome because they were metarational.

Clearly, however, the ad hoc nature of these explanations render them less general than the explanation derived from the equilibrium concepts associated with the theory of moves. Reminiscent of the deus ex machina of Greek tragedy, they are inferior because they are called upon if and only if the explana-

---

15. Nonmyopic equilibria exist in 37 of the 78 distinct 2 × 2 ordinal games identified by Rapoport and Guyer (1966). Of these 37 games, only two have a nonmyopic equilibria that are also not Nash equilibria. One of these is Prisoners' Dilemma. The other is Chicken. In both of these games, the cooperative outcome is stable in the nonmyopic sense but not in the sense of Nash. Thus, this dynamic equilibrium concept provides a rationale for cooperation in precisely the two games for which the question of cooperative behavior is the most salient and problematic.

16. See Zagare (1984, 17–21, 41) for such an interpretation.

tion based upon Nash's equilibrium concept is inadequate. By comparison, the ability of the concepts of a nonmyopic and a limited-move equilibrium to subsume the dynamics of the three games embedded in the 1967 Middle East crisis under-scores its essential utility, namely, the parsimony of explana-tion it brings to empirical analysis.

6

Evaluating the Cease-Fire Alert Decision of 1973

On October 25, 1973, President Richard M. Nixon ordered United States military forces to be put on a worldwide "precautionary alert," ostensibly to deter Soviet intervention to protect Egypt in the Yom Kippur War. Within hours after news of this order became public, the president and Secretary of State Henry Kissinger came under an intense attack by the American news media.[1]

Since the alert crisis followed less than a week after another politically controversial incident, the so-called Saturday Night Massacre in which the Watergate special prosecutor was fired and the attorney general and his top assistant resigned in protest, some critics of the administration suggested that "the alert might have been prompted as much perhaps by American domestic requirements as by the real requirements of diplomacy in the Middle East" (*New York Times,* October 26, 1973, p. 18). Others, accepting the administration's stated objectives, challenged the strategic wisdom of the president's action. For example, *Time* (November 5, 1973, p. 15) wondered whether "some less dramatic action might have ended the crisis," while a *New York Times* (October 29, 1973) editorial asked rhetorically, "What is the 'hot line' for, what are diplomats for?"

Adding to the general skepticism about the president's motives, as well as to the charge that the alert was an unnecessary overreaction, was the lack of solid evidence that the Soviets intended to intervene. When questioned, key administration

1. This chapter is based upon Frank C. Zagare, "A Game-Theoretic Evaluation of the Cease-Fire Alert Decision of 1973," *Journal of Peace Research* 20: 73–86.

officials were forced to admit that military moves taken by the Soviets just prior to the alert were, at best, "ambiguous" and did not differ significantly from actions taken by the Soviets earlier in the war.[2] Moreover, the administration was less than forthright about the contents of a personal letter from Soviet Communist Party General Secretary Leonid Brezhnev, warning of a unilateral Soviet initiative, that was cited by some as the specific precipitant of the crisis. Kissinger, for instance, though promising to release full documentation of the Soviet-American exchanges leading up to the confrontation "within a week or two," refused to discuss Brezhnev's note at his press conference the next day.[3] Nixon was equally evasive about the content of the letter, saying only that "it left very little to the imagination" (New York Times, October 27, 1973, p. 14).

Was the cease-fire alert a necessary diplomatic maneuver, or was it a needless overreaction and an avoidable provocation of the Soviet Union? In this chapter, I will attempt to answer this question, and indirectly, the political critics of the president, by examining the alert decision and asking what, if any, effect the American alert, presumably signaling a United States willingness to resist a Soviet intervention, had on the rational-strategy choice of the Soviet Union.

To this end, the background of the crisis, and the consequences of the choices facing Soviet and American decision-makers in October 1973, will be examined. Then, after evaluating the effect of the alert order on both the short-term and the long-term stability of the status quo, I will study an alternative strategy, suggested by critics of the decision. And finally, in the concluding section, the main arguments of this chapter will be summarized and extended.

2. For a detailed analysis of Soviet military moves prior to the alert crisis, see Glassman (1975, chap. 5).

3. Pointing to renewed superpower cooperation after the war, Kissinger later reneged on his promise to release the correspondence between Nixon and Brezhnev. A partial transcript of the Brezhnev note, though, appeared in the New York Times on April 10, 1974, p. 9.

6.1 The United States – Soviet Union Cease-Fire Game

The cease-fire alert decision has its origins in the October 1973 Middle East war. That war began on October 6, during the Jewish religious holiday of Yom Kippur, when Egypt and Syria, armed with Soviet weapons, attacked Israel, the closest ally of the United States in the Middle East.

The Arab attack caught both Israeli and American intelligence off guard and, as a result, Israel suffered initial losses on both the Egyptian and Syrian fronts. But by October 15, after a United States promise of a massive airlift of war matériel, the Israelis launched a counteroffensive, recapturing the Golan Heights and crossing over to the West Bank of the Suez Canal. For the next several days, the Israelis continued their advance, moving steadily toward Damascus and enlarging their flanking operation in Egypt, in the process threatening the supply lines of the Egyptian Third Army.

With both Egyptian and Syrian forces on the brink of disaster, a cease-fire agreement calling for direct negotiations between the two sides was worked out by the superpowers and accepted, albeit with some reluctance, by both the Arabs and the Israelis. Accordingly, on October 22, the United Nations Security Council unanimously adopted Resolution 338 calling for a cease-fire in place.

The original cease-fire, however, did not take hold, and the fighting continued. But before a second cease-fire could be arranged, the Israelis completed their encirclement of the Third Army. Thus, on October 24, faced with the destruction of his best fighting force, Egyptian President Anwar el-Sadat appealed to both the United States and the Soviet Union to send a joint peace-keeping force to police the October 22 cease-fire.

That evening, Soviet Ambassador Anatoly Dobrynin told Secretary of State Kissinger that the Soviet Union planned on introducing a resolution in the Security Council that would echo Sadat's appeal and involve both the Soviet Union and the United States in a peace-keeping operation (Kalb and Kalb 1974, 552–53). Shortly afterward, Nixon received the note from Brezhnev accusing Israel of flouting the cease-fire arrangement, demanding that a new cease-fire go into effect "without delay," and warning the United States president that "if you find it impossible to act together with us in this matter, we should be faced with the necessity urgently to consider the question of taking appropriate steps unilaterally. Israel cannot be allowed to get away with the violations" (*New York Times,* April 10, 1974).

Nixon responded, first, by ordering United States troops to be put on a worldwide alert, second, by sending Brezhnev a letter that reiterated his willingness to cooperate with the Soviets in promoting peace in the Middle East (Kalb and Kalb 1974, 556), and third, by delivering an ultimatum to the Israelis demanding that they permit the Third Army to be resupplied with nonmilitary equipment, food, and water (Dayan 1976, 544).[4]

By the following afternoon (October 25), the Soviets dropped their demand that Soviet *and* American troops be included in the peace-keeping operation, and the Security Council passed Resolution 340 which established a United Nations Emergency Force, that excluded Soviet and American participation, to enforce the October 22 cease-fire. Hence, on October 26, Nixon rescinded the alert order, and the superpower crisis, as well as the war in the Middle East, faded.

What effect did the United States alert have on the resolution of this conflict? To answer this question, the choices facing the two superpowers on October 24, their preferences regarding the consequences of these choices, and their perception of each other's preferences, must first be discussed.

The Possible Outcomes

At the time Sadat asked for United States and Soviet intervention, the two superpowers were faced with unusually difficult choices. With the Egyptian Third Army in an extremely

---

4. Compare this response with President Johnson's during the 1967 crisis.

vulnerable position, the Soviets had to decide whether to try to save it through normal diplomatic channels, or to accept Sadat's invitation and send a military contingent to protect it and the political position of the Egyptian government. For their part, United States decision-makers had to decide whether to cooperate with the Soviets in whatever way they chose to help Sadat, or to act to frustrate either a diplomatic or a military initiative by the Soviets.

Given these choices, four outcomes (summarized in figure 6.1) seemed possible on October 24:

A. *Compromise.* If the Soviets sought a diplomatic escape from Sadat's precarious position, and the United States cooperated with them by pressuring Israel to stop its advance and withdraw to the October 22 lines, the war would end, a superpower confrontation would be avoided, and their détente would be strengthened. In the Middle East, negotiations between Israel and the Arabs, as called for in Resolution 338, would perhaps begin to settle the long-simmering political disputes of the region.[5]

B. *Israeli Military Victory.* If the Soviets pursued a diplomatic solution to the conflict, while the United States blocked efforts in the United Nations to reimpose a cease-fire, or tacitly encouraged Israel to capture the Third Army, the Israelis would score a stunning military victory, Sadat's regime would most likely fall, and the Soviets would suffer a serious diplomatic setback in the region for abandoning Egypt.

C. *Soviet Victory.* If the Soviets and Americans agreed to Sadat's request for a joint peace-keeping force, or if the Soviets intervened unilaterally and the United States did nothing, the cease-fire of October 22 would be re-

5. Given the disposition of the Third Army on October 24, the compromise outcome constituted the status quo in this game.

SOVIET UNION

		Seek Diplomatic Solution	Intervene in War
UNITED STATES	**Cooperate with Soviet Initiative**	A. COMPROMISE. Egyptian Third Army resupplied; cease-fire of October 22 re-established; political resolution of Middle East conflict attempted.	C. SOVIET VICTORY. possible joint Soviet–American peace-keeping force; Soviet military presence in Middle East reintroduced.
	Frustrate Soviet Initiative	B. ISRAELI VICTORY. Possible occupation of Egypt, Syria, and Jordan.	D. SUPERPOWER CONFRONTATION.

FIGURE 6.1: Outcome Matrix for the Cease-fire Alert Game of 1973

imposed, the Egyptian Third Army would be rescued, and a Soviet military presence in the Middle East would be reestablished.

D. *Superpower Confrontation.* If the Soviets honored Sadat's call for help by intervening unilaterally, and the United States responded by sending troops to protect Israel's (and its own) position, combat troops of the two superpowers would be in close proximity and, in Nixon's (1978, 938) words, "an extremely dangerous potential for direct great power rivalry" would be introduced into the region.

American Preferences and Perceptions

As Rubinstein (1977, 275) correctly points out, "the question of whether the U.S. alert was an appropriate and necessary response to a threatened Soviet intervention can only be answered in light of how one assesses Soviet policy in the Middle East and Moscow's perceptions at the time." Accordingly, the following discussion will not seek to describe the actual objectives of the superpowers on October 24, but rather the *perception* of the United States leadership of (i) the Soviet preference order, and (ii) the Soviet's perception of the United States preference order.

Just before the alert order was given, there seemed to be very little debate among top United States decision-makers about Soviet objectives. It was generally thought that the Soviets most preferred to honor Sadat's request for a joint peace-keeping contingent to enforce Resolution 338 (outcome C).[6] "The Soviets would obviously back this idea," Nixon (1978, 937) later observed, because they viewed it "as an opportunity to reestablish their military presence in Egypt."

If the Soviets failed to achieve this objective, however, United States decision-makers believed that the Soviets preferred a compromise outcome (A) in which the pro-Soviet regimes in Egypt and Syria were preserved, to a possible military showdown with the United States (outcome D) that would spell the end of the superpower détente (Kalb and Kalb 1974, 547–48) and possibly escalate into war. Still, both Nixon (1978, 921) and Kissinger (Quandt 1977, 196) thought that the Soviets were prepared to risk such a confrontation rather than permit the Arabs to suffer a devastating defeat (outcome B). Thus, the Soviet preference order, as perceived by the United States leadership on October 24 was (C,A,D,B).[7]

What was the position of the Nixon administration during this crisis? When the war began, American decision-makers were hamstrung by their traditional loyalty and support of Israel and their desire not to alienate unduly the Arab states on

6. In fact, some analysts have argued that Sadat's request was orchestrated by the Soviets. For this opinion see, for example, Glassman (1975, 158).

7. Interestingly, most of those who criticized the alert decision on strategic grounds shared this perception. For an example, see Reston (1973b).

whose oil the United States was becoming increasingly dependent (Laquer 1974, 167; Quandt 1977, 177). The policy designed to accommodate these two conflicting constraints was the promotion of a military standoff (outcome A) rather than support of a sweeping Israeli victory in the war (outcome B) (Reston 1973a; Laquer 1974, 197). Or, as Nixon (1978, 921) put it:

> only a battlefield stalemate would provide the foundation on which fruitful negotiations might begin. Any equilibrium—even if only an equilibrium of mutual exhaustion—would make it easier to reach an enforceable settlement. Therefore, I was convinced that we must not use our influence to bring about a cease-fire that would leave the parties in such imbalance that negotiations for a permanent settlement would never begin.

In other words, the United States preferred outcome A to outcome B.

In turn, the Nixon administration preferred an Israeli military victory to either of the two outcomes (C and D) associated with Soviet intervention (Reston 1973a). Moreover, the United States leadership was firmly committed to resisting (outcome D) rather than acceding to a unilateral Soviet initiative (outcome C) (Nixon 1978, 922–24; Kissinger 1982, 580). Of course, the apparent United States preference for outcome D over C may have been a bluff, but in light of the high interests at stake, and the subsequent United States actions, this seems unlikely. Consequently, at the time of Sadat's call for a superpower-imposed armistice, the American preference order was (A,B,D,C).

How was the United States position perceived in Moscow? Despite almost constant high-level consultations between the two superpowers throughout this crisis, there is some evidence suggesting that the Soviets either misperceived, or were dubious of, stated American preferences, and that the Nixon administration was aware of this. For instance, a hot-line message from Brezhnev to Nixon on October 23 implied that the United States was colluding with Israel in violating the first cease-fire agreement (Nixon 1978, 936). And Secretary of Defense James Schlesinger was of the opinion that it was just such a Soviet misperception that prompted several "ambiguous" Soviet military moves just prior to the decision to alert United States combat forces (Quandt 1977, 199). If Brezhnev's note accurately reflected Soviet perceptions at the time, and Schlesinger was right, the Soviet leadership believed that the United States preferred outcome B to outcome A.[8]

Significantly, however, the Nixon administration did not appear preoccupied by this possible Soviet misperception, but rather was more concerned that the "crisis of confidence" resulting from the Watergate affair might have led the Soviet leadership to misinterpret the United States intention to come to Israel's rescue (outcome D) rather than accept a unilateral Soviet intervention (outcome C). Indeed, it was precisely the necessity to rectify this possible Soviet diagnosis of the American position that was cited as the purpose for the alert of United States troops on October 25. "Words were not making our point," Nixon (1978, 938) later wrote, "we needed action."[9]

6.2 The United States as Israel's Protector

If the Nixon administration's interpretation of Soviet preferences and perceptions is accepted, the psychological environment for the United States leadership on October 24 was defined by:

8. After all, just such a preference relationship was posited for the United States in the 1967 superpower game discussed in chapter 5.

9. More recently, Nixon has said "We could not allow the Soviets to have a predominant position in the region. That had to be the dominant line. I wanted to send that message, and putting the weapons on alert did that. We did not so much want to threaten the Soviet Union with nuclear weapons as to indicate that the U.S. would resist them, conventional and nuclear" (*Time*, July 29, 1985).

1. The four possible outcomes of the crisis (see figure 6.1);

2. Its perception of the Soviet preference order to be (C,A,D,B);

3. The Soviet (mis)perception of the American preference order to be (B,A,C,D).

This view of the superpower game, save for one exception to be noted shortly, is incorporated in the payoff matrices of figures 6.2 and 6.3.

The game of figure 6.2 (Called Bluff) represents the game that would have been played had the United States *not* alerted its troops. This variant of the superpower game reflects the Nixon administration's belief that the Soviets perceived an American preference to acquiesce to Soviet intervention rather than risk a military confrontation, that is, an American preference for outcome C over outcome D. It further assumes the Soviet perception of the United States as Israel's protector and sponsor, that is, a United States preference for outcome B over A.

The Prisoners' Dilemma game of figure 6.3 depicts the

| | | SOVIET UNION | |
		Seek Diplomatic Solution	Intervene in War
UNITED STATES	Cooperate with Soviet Initative	A. COMPROMISE (3,3)	C. SOVIET VICTORY (2,4)
	Frustrate Soviet Initiative	B. ISRAELI VICTORY (4,1)	D. CONFRONTATION (1,2)

FIGURE 6.2: The United States as Israel's Protector: Without Alert

SOVIET UNION

	Seek Diplomatic Solution	Intervene in War
Cooperate with Soviet Initiative	A. COMPROMISE (3,3)	C. SOVIET VICTORY (1,4)
Frustrate Soviet Initiative	B. ISRAELI VICTORY (4,1)	D. CONFRONTATION (2,2)

UNITED STATES (row label, at left between the two rows)

FIGURE 6.3: The United States as Israel's Protector: With Alert

same situation as figure 6.2, except to posit a United States preference to resist (outcome D) rather than acquiesce (outcome C) to a Soviet intervention. Since both Nixon and Kissinger claimed that the alert order was intended to signal a United States intention to oppose the introduction of Soviet forces into the Middle East, it will be assumed that the salient environmental change brought about by the alert order was to transform the United States–Soviet Union game from Called Bluff to Prisoners' Dilemma.

What effect did the alert of the United States forces have on the decision of the Soviet Union not to intervene in the October war? The answer to this question, of course, lies ultimately in whether an incentive existed for the Soviets to intervene in the game that would have been played had the alert order not been given (see figure 6.2), and whether or not the rational strategy choice of the Soviet Union was in any way different in the game actually played (see figure 6.3). Therefore, to gauge the effect of the alert on Soviet behavior, both the short-term and the long-term stability of the compromise outcome in figures 6.2 and 6.3 must be examined. In what follows, short-term stability will be measured by Nash's equilibrium concept, while Brams and Wittman's concept of a nonmyopic equilibrium will be used to monitor long-term stability.

By comparing figure 6.2 with figure 6.3, one can see that when the United States is assumed to be Israel's protector, the short-term stability of the status quo (outcome A) is not affected by the change in United States preferences implied by the alert order. For, since the Soviets prefer outcome C to outcome A in both games, they have an immediate incentive to move away from the status quo (their second most-preferred alternative) to outcome C (their most-preferred alternative), regardless of the preference order announced by the United States.

What does change in the short-run with the alert order, though, is the implied outcome of the game and the rational-strategy choice of the United States. In figure 6.2, if the Soviets move away from the status quo, the rational strategy of the United States, associated with the unique Nash equilibrium, (2,4), is to cooperate with the Soviets and perhaps join them in a joint peace-keeping operation. On the other hand, in figure 6.3, if the Soviets departed from the status quo, the rational strategy of the United States, associated with the unique Nash equilibrium in this game (2,2), is to back Israel and challenge the Soviet intervention.

It is clear, then, that under this interpretation of the game, short-term factors cannot provide a justification for the United States alert decision since the rational-strategy choice of the Soviet Union remained the same both before (figure 6.2) and after (figure 6.3) the alert order was given. Moreover, the concept of a Nash equilibrium is not very useful for either describing or explaining the dynamics of this game. Since the status quo is not a Nash equilibrium in figure 6.3, Nash's equilibrium concept cannot explain the stability of the compromise outcome in the game actually played. And since the strategies finally chosen by the United States and the Soviet Union do not correspond to the unique Nash equilibrium in this game,

Nash's equilibrium concept cannot explain superpower behavior during the alert crisis.

All of this changes, however, when the long-term stability of the status quo is examined in these two variants of the United States–Soviet Union game. For a demonstration of this, consider now figure 6.4, which lists the sequence of choices and counterchoices implied by a departure of the Soviet Union from (3,3) in figure 6.2.

The last choice open to the players in figure 6.4, before cycling back to the original status quo occurs, is that of the United States.[10] At this node, the United States is faced with a choice of staying at (4,1), its best outcome, or switching back to (3,3), its second-best outcome. Clearly, should this node be reached in a series of moves and countermoves, the United States would (rationally) stay at (4,1).[11]

Assuming, then, that the United States would stay, what should the Soviet Union decide at the node immediately preceding the United States choice at (4,1)? At this node, the Soviets are faced with a choice of staying at (1,2), their next-worst outcome, or moving to (4,1), their worst outcome, where the game would end. Given such a choice, the Soviets would rationally stay at (1,2).

Would the Soviets ever have to make this decision? To determine this, consider the United States choice leading to it. At the node immediately preceding the Soviet choice at (1,2), the United States must choose between staying at (2,4), its next-worst outcome, or moving to its worst outcome at (1,2). Again, if the United States anticipates the rational Soviet choice at the next move, it will rationally choose to stay at (2,4).

Finally, should the Soviets move away from the original status quo at (3,3) to outcome C at (2,4)? If the Soviets moved to (2,4), the United States would rationally choose to stay there, and the game would end. Given its preference for (2,4)

10. The reader who is comfortable with this algorithm may prefer to skip the next five paragraphs.
11. Thus, there is *termination* of the sequential move process in this game.

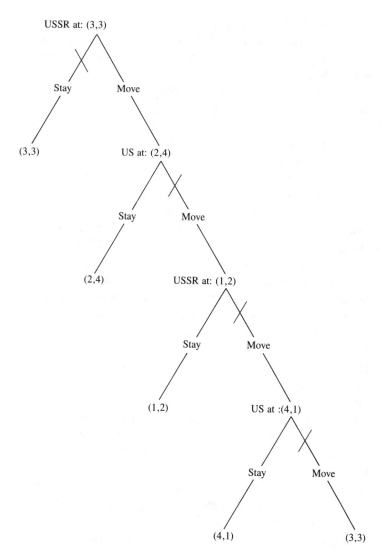

FIGURE 6.4: Game Tree of the Called Bluff Variant of the Superpower Game, Given an Initial Departure by the Soviet Union

over (3,3), therefore, the rational Soviet choice would be to change its strategy and accept Sadat's appeal for help. Hence, in this representation of the superpower game, the status quo is not stable in the nonmyopic sense since one player (i.e., the Soviet Union) can induce a better outcome by unilaterally departing from it and changing its strategy.[12]

Once the Soviets depart from the status quo to outcome C, though, neither player would have an incentive to switch strategies again. Since outcome C is the best outcome for the Soviet Union, it is clear that it would have nothing to gain by changing its strategy again. Similarly, as was just illustrated, the United States does better by staying at (2,4) than by moving away from it. And because both players prefer outcome C to the outcome rationally implied by a series of moves and countermoves away from it, (2,4) is a nonmyopic equilibrium.

A nonmyopic analysis of the game of figure 6.2, then, is remarkably similar to an analysis based upon Nash's equilibrium notion. The status-quo outcome (A) is not stable in either the Nash or nonmyopic sense in figure 6.2, whereas outcome C is stable in both the Nash and the nonmyopic sense. Hence, if this game were played, both equilibrium concepts would predict outcome (C), the most-preferred alternative of the Soviet Union and the next-worst alternative of the United States, as the outcome that would be chosen by rational players.

The two equilibrium concepts part company, however, when the Prisoners' Dilemma game of figure 6.3 is examined. Although the status quo is not a Nash equilibrium in this game, it is, of course, a nonmyopic equilibrium. Consequently, only long-term considerations can provide a justification (or explanation) for the United States alert on October 25; and since both players ultimately chose a strategy supporting the status quo, only the concept of a nonmyopic equilibrium can account

12. By contrast, the United States does not have an incentive to depart from the status quo in the game depicted in figure 6.2 since a strategy switch would only induce a less-preferred outcome, i.e., (2,4).

for the actual strategies selected by the United States and the Soviet Union in this game.

The extremely fragile nature of the (3,3) outcome in Prisoners' Dilemma was discussed in the last chapter. Recall that not only is the conflictual outcome (2,2) also stable in the non-myopic sense, but it is also the outcome that is implied by a sequence of moves and countermoves from any outcome, other than (3,3), in this game. Thus, if the Soviets had interpreted the American alert decision as the first step in an actual strategy change for the United States (from restraining Israel to supporting an Israeli military victory) rather than as intended (as a limited statement of an American preference for outcome D over outcome C), they may have been tempted to preempt the United States strategy or send troops to rescue Sadat. As is clear, however, a Soviet intervention in the Middle East rationally implies an American counterintervention, and with it, the very real possibility of a nuclear war.

In light of the above, one can certainly understand those who criticized the strategic wisdom of the alert order. When the Nixon administration placed United States forces on alert, it was playing a very dangerous game indeed. One must question, therefore, whether a decision that Kissinger letter described as a "deliberate overreaction" was worth the risk of Armageddon, or whether a less provocative action might have achieved the same result. This question will be addressed next.

6.3 The United States as Honest Broker: Détente versus Realpolitik

What form would such an alternative strategy take? A more prudent, less provocative, and less dangerous tactic that might also have deterred Soviet intervention, according to Glassman (1975, 65) was the following: "rather than declaring a meaningless alert and putting pressure on Israel, a better response to the Russian threats might have been a diplomatic statement that the United States was also concerned with implementing a ceasefire and that we would seek to convince Israel of the necessity of such a move." [13]

In game-theoretic terms, Glassman's alternative strategy can be interpreted to mean a call for a United States announcement that it preferred to promote a compromise outcome (A) rather than an Israeli military victory (outcome B), that is, that it wished to play the role of mediator or honest broker in the war. [14] As already indicated, this was the actual position of the Nixon administration, and the Soviets were skeptical of it. Thus, this suggestion might be rejected on the grounds that the Soviet leadership would probably not have taken such a statement seriously. Nevertheless, there is also some chance that a dramatic announcement by Nixon or Kissinger might have altered the Soviet perception of the United States position. [15] If this were the case, would a statement of an American preference to promote a Middle East stalemate have been sufficient to deter Soviet intervention?

To answer this question, consider the representation of the superpower game depicted in figure 6.5. This game is the game that would have been played had the United States taken Glassman's advice. It assumes both a United States preference for outcome A over B, and the (mistaken) Soviet perception of an American preference for outcome C over outcome D. [16]

13. Glassman goes on to say, though, that "the United States could not consider employing its influence under the threat or reality of Soviet intervention."

14. Although it may seem odd that the outcome labeled "compromise" is the most-preferred outcome of one of the players in this game, I will continue to use this name for outcome A for the sake of consistency.

15. President Kennedy's television statement that marked the beginning of the Cuban missile crisis for the Soviet Union is one example in which such an action had this kind of effect.

16. The following argument is not affected by this assumption. As will be seen, the status quo is neither a nonmyopic nor a Nash equilibrium in the game of figure 6.5, nor would it be if an American preference for outcome D over C is assumed. It is important to note that figure 6.5 can also be interpreted as an alternative representation of the superpower game on October 24. If this was the game that was actually played, the alert decision could not be justified on strategic grounds since it did not enhance either the short-term or the long-term stability of the compromise outcome.

FIGURE 6.5: The United States as Honest Broker

Since this representation of the superpower game assumes the same preferences for the Soviet Union as previously postulated, the short-term incentive of the Soviet Union to honor Sadat's request for help remains unchanged. As before, the compromise outcome is not a Nash equilibrium.

Consequently, the key question in evaluating Glassman's prescription becomes whether or not his recommended strategy is as successful in removing the long-term incentive of the Soviets to intervene and, at the same time, is less risky than the decision to place American troops on alert.

The short answer to this question is "no." In figure 6.5, outcome A is not a nonmyopic equilibrium. Moreover, since at least one player has an incentive to depart from every outcome, each outcome is rendered unstable in the nonmyopic sense (see the arrows in figure 6.5). In other words, the process of moves and countermoves is intransitive, that is, it leads to cycling among the four possible outcomes. As a result, one must conclude that this alternative tactic is not as successful in eliminating the incentive of the Soviet Union to intervene in the October War as was the tactic of placing United States forces on alert.

Recall from chapter 3, though, that if one assumes that the revisionist player (i.e., the Soviet Union) in this game of unilateral deterrence prefers to accept its next-best outcome in order to avoid the possibility of cycling among the four possible outcomes, the status quo becomes an absorbing, or almost nonmyopically stable, outcome, and that the process of alternating strategy choices will lead rationally to, or converge upon, the status quo.[17] This suggests that the viability of the strategy suggested by Glassman and others rests ultimately on the faith one places in the pledge of the Soviet leaders not to seek unilateral advantages in such a crisis situation, that is, in the strength of the détente relationship itself. But as a consequence of both the tone and the content of Brezhnev's note, both Nixon and Kissinger placed a high probability on the likelihood that the Soviets would intervene and void the détente agreement (Kalb and Kalb 1974, 555).[18]

It is not surprising, then, that the Nixon administration decided not to place its faith in détente (or Soviet self-restraint), but instead chose to rely on a strategy rooted in the venerable tradition of realpolitik, even though this strategy entailed certain risks. Game-theoretically speaking, the administration's decision was sound and understandable. The long-term stability of the status quo in the game induced by the alert order (see figure 6.3) does not depend upon either wishful thinking or the benevolence of Soviet leaders, but rather depends upon Soviet recognition of their own interests.

By contrast, an announcement by the United States that it was interested in compromise is not sufficient to remove all long-term incentives of the Soviets to upset the status quo. Consequently, the choice of United States decision-makers was not only rational but also revealed the faith they placed, when push came to shove, in détente, a policy that had come to sym-

17. For a demonstration, see section 3.2.
18. By contrast, Secretary of Defense Schlesinger thought this probability to be "quite low" (*Department of State Bulletin,* November 19, 1973, p. 623).

bolize the Nixon administration in foreign affairs. Or as Nixon (1978, 941) himself later put it:

> I evaluated the Soviet behavior during the Mideast crisis not as an example of the failure of detente but as an illustration of its limitations—limitations of which I had always been keenly aware. I told the bipartisan leadership meeting on October 25, "I have never said that the Soviets are 'good guys'. What I have always said is that we should not enter into unnecessary confrontations with them." The Soviet Union will always act in its own self-interest; and so will the United States. Détente cannot change that.[19]

6.4 Summary and Conclusions

This chapter uses a game-theoretic framework to evaluate the decision of the Nixon administration to place United States forces on a worldwide alert to deter Soviet intervention in the October 1973 war in the Middle East. It finds that the alert decision can be justified and explained if the Nixon administration's perception of the game is accepted, but only when the long-term rationality of Soviet decision-makers is assumed. It also finds that a less provocative strategy, such as approaching the Soviet leadership and reasserting an American willingness to compromise, would have produced a more tenuous stability than that produced by the alert decision, and that the equilibrium resulting from this alternative policy rested upon a degree of trust that the Soviets would not seek unilateral advantage in the conflict.

The positive role that Prisoners' Dilemma games play in the resolution of international conflict is confirmed by the analysis of the 1973 alert crisis. This possibility has not previously been recognized or appreciated, except by those analysts who

19. At his news conference on October 26, however, Nixon claimed that his détente policy was responsible for the peaceful resolution of the crisis (*New York Times*, October 27, 1973, p. 14).

point out that third parties outside the game may benefit when players in this game fail to cooperate (see, for instance, Luce and Raiffa 1957, 97). Moreover, as suggested in chapter 2, since a compromise rooted in a strategy of realpolitik in a Prisoners' Dilemma game is more stable, in a dynamic sense at least, than a compromise rooted in a détente relationship that rests upon the shaky foundation of prior "agreements" or "understandings," farsighted players seeking to avoid conflict, and simultaneously seeking to promote their own interests, may have an incentive to create, rather than avoid, Prisoners' Dilemma games.

Indeed, not only do such considerations provide a rationale for the alert decision, but they also plausibly explain Soviet military moves, culminating in Brezhnev's note to Nixon, just prior to the alert of American forces. Soviet actions at this time were most likely aimed at convincing United States and Israeli decision-makers that the Soviet leadership preferred to fight rather than accept an Israeli military victory (Rubinstein 1977, 276). It is possible, therefore, that the policies of both superpowers were directed at reinforcing the Prisoners' Dilemma structure of the crisis in order to avoid the consequences of losing a game of Called Bluff.

7

Analyzing the U.S.-USSR Strategic Relationship

The purpose of this chapter is to offer a parsimonious and logically consistent evaluation of the strategic relationship of the United States and the Soviet Union from 1945 to date (1986). Perhaps the most notable feature of the superpower relationship during this period has been the absence of a general war between these two most powerful actors in the international system. Significantly, the observed stability of this relationship has persisted despite the fact that most strategic analysts agree that there have been several moments of potential or theoretical instability since 1945, as the overall balance of power, assessed chiefly in terms of the capabilities of each side, has shifted from one of an American nuclear monopoly, and then superiority, to one of approximate parity or essential equivalence.

All of which raises an interesting question: what emendations in existent strategic theory are necessary to reconcile the actual stability of the postwar nuclear period with the moments of instability postulated by deterrence theorists? I will attempt to answer this question by embedding an analysis of the superpower relationship in the theory of moves framework and asking what assumptions about each side's capabilities, preferences, and perceptions are consistent with the absence of a strategic war between the United States and the Soviet Union.[1]

1. A game-theoretic approach in general, and the theory of moves in particular, is particularly suited for answering questions of this sort. As Muzzio (1982, 152) has pointed out, the power of game theory "lies not only in the fact that we can use it to provide a point of view, and to organize information around it, but also to discriminate among various motivational assumptions that work and do not work to explain the events that occurred."

**TABLE 7.1: Mutual Deterrence and the Superpower Strategic
          Relationship**

Credible threat	Equal Power	U.S. Is Predominant
Both credible (Prisoners' Dilemma)	stable mutual deterrence	stable mutual deterrence
U.S. only (Called Bluff)	U.S. victory	U.S. victory
USSR only (Called Bluff)	USSR victory	USSR victory
Neither credible (Chicken)	stable mutual deterrence *	U.S. victory

Key: *Depends upon the ability of the players to pass through (a_2, b_2).

Although there are no clear-cut objective criteria that can
be used to divide the postwar era into more manageable time
periods, there is an underlying consensus in the literature that
several distinct stages, separated by different combinations
of strategic capabilities, have existed in the superpower relationship. The following division is representative of this
consensus and will be used as the basis for the subsequent
discussion: 1. 1945–50, the period of American nuclear
monopoly; 2. 1951–55, the first period of U.S. superiority;
3. 1956–61, the period of mutual vulnerability; 4. 1962–66,
the second period of U.S. superiority; and 5. 1967 to date, the
period of essential equivalence.[2]

7.1 Summarizing the Model

For the convenience of the reader, the principal conclusions
drawn from a theory-of-moves analysis of the strategic relationship of the United States and the Soviet Union are summarized in tables 7.1 and 7.2 respectively. Each table controls for
two different power configurations and the four logically pos-

2. See, for instance, Quester (1970), Kahan (1975), Russett (1983), or Smoke
(1984).

TABLE 7.2: Unilateral Deterrence and the Superpower Strategic Relationship

Credible Threat	U.S. is a status-quo power USSR is a revisionist power		U.S. is a revisionist power USSR is a status-quo power	
	Equal Power	U.S. Is Predominant	Equal Power	U.S. Is Predominant
Both credible [game 64(48)]	stable deterrence if USSR is risk-averse; otherwise indeterminate	USSR is deterred	stable deterrence if U.S. is risk-averse; otherwise indeterminate	U.S. is deterred
U.S. only [game 76(72) or 15(21)]	stable deterrence if USSR is risk-averse; otherwise indeterminate	USSR is deterred	stable deterrence if U.S. is risk-averse; otherwise indeterminate	U.S. victory
USSR only [game 15(21) or 76(72)]	stable deterrence if USSR is risk-averse; otherwise indeterminate	USSR victory	stable deterrence if U.S. is risk-averse; otherwise indeterminate	U.S. is deterred
Neither credible [game 65(55)]	stable deterrence if USSR is risk-averse; otherwise indeterminate	USSR is deterred	stable deterrence if U.S. is risk-averse; otherwise indeterminate	U.S. victory

sible assumptions that can be made about the credibility of each player's threat. Table 7.1 posits a game of mutual deterrence while table 7.2 assumes a relationship of unilateral deterrence.

Two important qualifications about the deductions listed in these tables are in order. First, all of the listed conclusions rest upon the assumption that each player has, at a minimum, a second-strike capability, that is, the ability to respond should the other player move from the status quo. (When more stringent assumptions are required to generate these findings, the precise nature of the requisite assumptions is indicated in the table notes.) And second, under certain conditions, almost all of these results can be disturbed. Since both tables would be unduly complicated if every possible exception were noted, and since only a few of these disturbances are relevant to the subsequent discussion, they will be considered on an individual basis, but only when they have a bearing on the topic at hand.

7.2 The American Nuclear Monopoly: 1945–50

In the most literal sense of the word, the postwar era was ushered in with a bang. For all intents and purposes, the old world order disappeared when the United States dropped an atomic bomb on Hiroshima and another on Nagasaki in August 1945. Both Germany and Japan were defeated; all that remained was for the victors to divide the spoils.

The postwar international system differed in two fundamental respects from the prewar system. First, it was bipolar rather than multipolar and, second, it was nuclear. These two characteristics of the present international system have been the essential constants of the division of spoils games played by the United States and the Soviet Union ever since 1945.

As was to be expected, when the Axis powers were finally defeated, both the United States and the Soviet Union started to demobilize. The Soviet demobilization, however, was gradual and partial. By contrast, the American reductions were, for a variety of reasons, faster and more complete. Most analysts agree that the American demobilization created a power vacuum in Europe. Given the dominance of Soviet conventional forces on the Continent, the Soviets could, in effect, hold Europe "hostage." This threat to Western Europe constituted the principle source of Soviet leverage against possible coercive threats from the United States.

The Americans, of course, had the bomb. While few doubted that it was better to have nuclear weapons than not, "it is remarkable how little military and political importance was attached to the early atomic bomb by many Western observers at the time" (Quester 1970, 1). The reasons for this are varied. To begin with, the American stockpile of nuclear weapons was very small (Rosenberg 1983); in addition, the assessment by many in the Truman administration that the strategic bombing programs against both Germany and Japan had been a failure undermined the opinion that the United States could have quickly and decisively defeated the Soviet Union in an armed conflict (Freedman 1981). Moreover, the "bring the boys home" riots in 1945 that were partially responsible for the rapid American demobilization underscored the fact that a preventive war against the Soviet Union would probably be without the popular support necessary to wage a war of attrition against the Soviets (Manchester 1973).

Given these considerations, the general shape of the game played during this initial period took form: the superpower game would be played between one player with a monopoly of nuclear weapons (i.e., the United States) and another player with obvious conventional superiority in the only theater that really mattered, Europe. In a game in which neither side could confidently claim to be preponderant, then, each player had two broad choices, either to accept the postwar status quo or to vigorously attempt to upset it. The four outcomes associated with these choices are summarized verbally in figure 7.1.

SOVIET UNION

	b_1	b_2
a_1	Postwar status quo maintained. (a_1, b_1)	Soviets overrun Western Europe; Balance of power favors USSR. (a_1, b_2)
a_2	US dominant; Soviets lose control of Eastern Europe. (a_2, b_1)	Global war. (a_2, b_2)

(Row labels under **UNITED STATES**: a_1, a_2)

FIGURE 7.1: The Superpower Game, Circa Late 1945

If there is major disagreement in the strategic literature about the game played by the superpowers during this period, it is not about the nature of the choices and the likely outcomes that the players faced. Differences of opinion exist, and fundamental ideological orientations begin to intrude into evaluations of this period, in the interpretation of the preferences of the two players over the set of outcomes. Accordingly, the consistency of some of these interpretations with both the deductions of the formal model presented herein and with the empirical record will now be evaluated.

Though the possibility is seldom discussed in strategic evaluations of this period, one possible explanation for the stability of the international system in the immediate postwar era, and for all subsequent periods, is a preference of both sides for the status quo that evolved after 1945. Despite the fact that most commentators argue that either the United States or the Soviet Union emerged from the Second World War desiring no more than the consolidation of the fruits of its victory, it is within the realm of the possible that each side, at least initially, was content with Hitler's elimination and hoped that a modus vivendi could be worked out with the other.

In terms of the deterrence game summarized in figure 7.1, this interpretation of the preferences of the superpowers implies that both preferred (a_1, b_1) to any other outcome. Clearly, were this the case, the status quo would have been the unique (Nash or nonmyopic) equilibrium outcome in this game, thereby rendering any competition, or attempts at deterrence, largely superfluous. Of course, a perception by each side that the other was not satisfied with the prevailing status quo is also necessary to explain much of the resultant behavior. Nevertheless, whatever steps either side took to deter the other, the hypothesis that both sides were more or less content to divide the world into their respective spheres of influence immediately after the defeat of Germany is consistent with the empirical record and the deductions of the model.

A second possible interpretation of the game played during this period posits asymmetric motivations to the two players. Specifically, one side or the other is assumed to be a satisfied status-quo player while the other is characterized as an unsatisfied revisionist player. For instance, Howard (1983) has argued that the Soviet Union was essentially concerned with preserving the postwar status quo at this time[3] while the United States was not. The more prevalent assumption, at least in the Western literature, reverses this argument (see, for instance, Brodie 1959; Intriligator and Brito 1984, 82).

Howard's premise that the Soviet Union was status-quo oriented during this period, while the United States was not, does not, by itself, explain the stability of the 1945–51 period. From table 7.2 it can be seen that if a more or less equal distribution of military power is postulated, then Howard's assumption must be augmented by the additional assumption that the Truman administration was risk-averse in order to be rendered

3. Howard characterizes the Soviet Union as a status-quo power until 1955.

sufficient for explaining the absence of war at this time. Conversely, if the United States is assumed to be the only satisfied player, then Soviet risk-aversion must be posited if the stability of this period is to be accounted for.

The argument that the stability of the 1945–50 era can be attributed to risk-averse behavior by the superpowers is not an uncommon one in the strategic literature. In fact, some students of international politics have even suggested that prudent crisis-management techniques have been responsible for the absence of war for the entire postwar period (Williams 1975). Superpower behavior during the 1948 Berlin crisis, the most dramatic confrontation of this time, is frequently pointed to as a case in point. For instance, during this crisis President Truman is said to have rejected General Clay's proposal to send an armored column to Berlin to break the blockade on the grounds that this action was too risky. Even the official Soviet explanation for the imposition of the blockade, i.e., that there were "technical difficulties" with the railroad lines and other transportation facilities leading to Berlin, has been characterized as an example of extremely circumspect behavior since this excuse "left the way open for retreat without sacrifice of principle, if retreat should be desirable" (Davison 1958, 71).

Too much weight, however, should not be placed on evidence of this sort. Observations about superpower behavior that are used to explain or predict superpower behavior surely involve a great deal of circular reasoning. Moreover, such anecdotal evidence conflicts with what is, to my knowledge, the only extant measure, independent of the behavior to be predicted, of the risk-taking propensities of the superpowers (Bueno de Mesquita, 1985b).[4] These data indicate that the Soviet leadership was indeed risk-averse vis-à-vis the United States in Europe during 1946 and 1947, but that, from 1948 on, the Soviets have been risk-acceptant. Parenthetically, such a finding is consistent with the fact that the Soviets did choose

---

4. For a detailed discussion of this measure, see Bueno de Mesquita (1985a).

to precipitate a crisis with the West over Berlin in 1948. Thus, the conventional wisdom that Soviet leaders have traditionally been loath to take risks (see, for instance, Triska and Finley 1968) is at odds with at least one theoretically derived set of indicators.

Bueno de Mesquita's risk measures also reveal the American leadership to be risk-averse vis-à-vis the Soviets, but only through 1948. Since that time, the competition between the superpowers has truly been a "competition in risk taking" (Schelling 1960). Thus, while it is possible to attribute the absence of a general war in 1946 and 1947 to the fact that one or the other superpower was disinclined to take risks to advance its interests, this proposition is without systematically collected empirical support after 1948.

A third possibility is that both the United States and the Soviet Union were unsatisfied with the status quo immediately after World War II, thereby rendering the game they played a game of mutual deterrence. It is not difficult to construct a strong case to support this particular argument. For instance, as Gaddis (1982) has persuasively argued, one dimension of George Kennan's conceptualization of his "containment strategy" involved the attempted fragmentation of the international communist movement, with the ultimate aim of weakening the power base of the Soviet Union. By definition, a satisfied status-quo power would not be motivated to take steps toward the elimination of a rival power. Moreover, it also seems plausible to entertain the assumption that as the number-two power in the international system, the Soviet Union, while desiring to consolidate its postwar gains, would also have preferred, ceteris paribus, a slightly more advantageous settlement and division of spoils.

Manifestly, however, if both the United States and the Soviet Union are assumed to be revisionist players, limits must be placed upon the extent of their dissatisfaction with the status quo in order to explain the absence of a superpower war at this time. For instance, if either side was so dissatisfied that it preferred war to the status quo [i.e., (a_2,b_2) to (a_1,b_1)], deterrence is not stable. In this case, the extremely unsatisfied power's non-status-quo strategy would have been *strictly dominant* since its two best outcomes would have been associated with this strategy. Thus, on both logical and empirical grounds, this interpretation, and each of its logically possible variants, can be rejected. (See chapter 4 for a more detailed explanation.)

There are, nevertheless, two assumptions about the preferences of the superpowers that are consistent with the possibility that each side was unhappy with the post-1945 status quo and the observation that neither side made a major effort to upset it. For instance, from table 7.1 it can be seen that mutual deterrence is stable if each side has a capable and credible retaliatory threat. The reason why deterrence is stable under these conditions is that while each side would prefer to replace the prevailing status quo with a more agreeable order, each side also preferred the status quo to going to war to alter it. And if each player's threat is perceived to be credible, each power would anticipate that the other would resist any attempt to manipulate the postwar lines of demarcation.

It is worth pointing out that Soviet declaratory policy during this period is particularly consistent with this explanation for the stability of the superpower relationship. Since the United States enjoyed a monopoly of nuclear weapons, the Soviets had to convince the United States leadership that they did not consider this asymmetry to be decisive. Put in a slightly different way, given a credible retaliatory threat by the United States, stable mutual deterrence depended upon the perception of the Truman administration that the Soviet threat to Western Europe was also credible, that is, that the Soviets preferred (a_2,b_2) to (a_2,b_1). Clearly, such a perception could not be maintained if the American nuclear monopoly was acknowledged to be decisive. Consequently, regardless of whether or not the Soviets believed their own propaganda, strategic reasons existed for expecting that the propaganda would take precisely the form that it did.

The second interpretation of superpower preferences that is consistent with the observed stability of this period, and with the argument that each player was dissatisfied with the status quo, requires the assumption that *neither* player's threat was perceived to be credible. Under these conditions deterrence is stable since, without a clear power advantage, neither player could have been sure of inducing a better outcome by switching to its non-status-quo strategy. The reason for this is that if one player moved from the status quo, the other could always respond by countermoving to mutual confrontation, i.e., (a_2,b_2), thereby forcing the player that initially departed from the status quo to choose between its worst and next-worst outcome as the final outcome of the game. By contrast, by not moving, each player ensures its next-best outcome, the original status quo.

It should be emphasized, however, that this interpretation of systemic stability depends upon the most general set of rules associated with the theory of moves, that is, for the status quo to remain stable under these conditions, both players must be able to move *to,* and *through,* mutual confrontation. But given the absence of a clear-cut first-strike capability by either side, and the fact that only a limited number of nuclear weapons were possessed by the United States at this time, it seems safe to assume that these conditions were met. Hence, on both logical and empirical grounds, this particular hypothesis cannot be rejected.

One popular proposition about the causes of international stability from 1945 to 1951 is somewhat difficult to interpret in terms of the deterrence model developed herein, namely, the argument that peace ensued only because the American leadership eschewed the possibility of a preventive war. There are two variants of this argument. The first attributes the lack of an American military initiative to the naiveté of the Truman administration, and the second to a strong moral imperative and abhorrence of war traditional of American elites (Smoke 1984). Both of these explanations rest upon the assumption that the American nuclear monopoly conferred a clear military advantage upon the United States. It is important to remember that this assessment of the military value of nuclear weapons was questioned not only by Soviet propagandists but also by many in the upper circles of the American executive branch (Quester 1970).

In light of the debate about the nature of the American military advantage, the hypothesis that strategic blunders and leadership incompetence were responsible for the peaceful conditions after World War II is best interpreted as a normative proposition resting upon a dubious empirical base. Recast, it is best stated as an injunction: the United States should have attacked the Soviet Union since it was almost assuredly guaranteed victory. Needless to say, this argument conveniently overlooks the fact that the costs associated with such a "victory" were perceived by most American decision-makers to outweigh the benefits, so that even if American military supremacy is accepted, the preference of the Truman administration for (a_1, b_1) over (a_2, b_2) is understandable.

For the proposition attributing stability to the moral character of the United States leadership to make sense, similar assumptions about American preferences must also be made, that is, it must be assumed that an American victory over the Soviet Union was guaranteed and that the benefits of winning a war against the Soviets outweighed the costs, save for the moral dimension that produced a United States preference for (a_1, b_1) over (a_2, b_2) or even (a_2, b_1).

Both of these propositions, then, stand on an equivalent logical foundation. They both posit, though they evaluate differently, an American preference for the status quo over war, and they both assume an American military advantage. Since there are several interpretations of the model consistent with each of these explanations, neither can be rejected on logical or empirical grounds.

7.3 The First Period of American Strategic Superiority: 1951–55

The first period of the strategic relationship of the United States and the Soviet Union began to give way in 1949, although the salient features of the succeeding period did not fully emerge until the first year of the Eisenhower administration. In 1949, the Soviets detonated their first (detected) nuclear device and United States decision-makers set in motion plans for a huge conventional buildup that would soon dissipate the lopsided advantage enjoyed by the Soviets during the first period. Nevertheless, by themselves, neither of these alterations in the strategic environment were far-reaching enough to alter the essential characteristics of the superpower game. What distinguished the second from the first period was the clear and large advantage of the United States by 1951 and the years that followed in both nuclear weapons and strategic delivery vehicles (Kahan 1975, 27). Even though the American nuclear monopoly had been broken, and even though the Soviets were about to beat the United States to the punch in testing a deliverable thermonuclear device (Quester 1970, 92), the American strategic advantage was evident. Whereas previously the limited size of the American nuclear arsenal raised questions about its efficacy in a war of industrial attrition with the Soviet Union, now the sheer number of nuclear weapons possessed by the United States, coupled with the ability to deliver them from SAC bases in both the United States and Europe, and the inability of the Soviets to respond in kind, ushered in an era of unquestioned American strategic superiority (Quester 1970, 89; Hopkins and Mansbach 1973, 384; Kahan 1975, chap. 1; Russett 1983, 8–11; Smoke 1984, chap. 5).

While the American strategic advantage was obvious in 1951, so was the realization that it would be short-lived. One 1952 study, for instance, guessed that the Soviets would have about 130 nuclear warheads in their arsenal by 1953 and that this number would grow to 200 by 1954 and to 270 by 1955 (Quester 1970, 77). In and of themselves, however, these numbers did not necessarily pose a threat to the position of dominance enjoyed by the United States. At this time, the Soviet bomber fleet still did not possess the round-trip capability necessary to wage an extended war against the United States. Nevertheless, the expected development of thermonuclear weapons would soon render implausible both a war of attrition and a limited-war scenario. Consequently, in the not too distant future, the inability of Soviet Tu-4s and later intermediate-range Soviet bombers to strike the United States and return home for reloading would be, strategically speaking, of little moment. In other words, the full flowering of the nuclear age, in which the United States would be vulnerable to either a pre-emptive or retaliatory blow by the Soviet Union, could be anticipated to evolve shortly.

Given the defining characteristics of the 1951–55 period, and assuming that its strategic capability conferred a power advantage on the United States, there are several interpretations of the deterrence model consistent with the observed stability of this period. As can be seen from table 7.2, three of these interpretations are associated with the assumption that the United States was a status-quo power. As long as it has a credible threat, or the revisionist player lacks one, a status-quo power with recognizable military superiority should deter a weaker revisionist state since its power advantage removes any incentive the revisionist player might have to depart from the status quo. Under these conditions, a preponderant status-quo player will rationally respond to a move away from the status quo by the revisionist player since, by resisting, it will induce a better outcome than the outcome that would be induced should it not resist. Conversely, unless the status-quo player lacks a credible threat and the revisionist player does not, the final outcome in a deterrence game in which the more powerful player responds to a deviation from the status quo by the weaker player will always be worse for the weaker (i.e., the revisionist) player. As a result, deterrence is stable under these conditions.

Was the United States status-quo orientated during this period or was it interested in promoting a "rollback" of the Soviet position in Eastern Europe, as some Republicans suggested during the presidential campaign? It is, of course, impossible to give a definitive answer to this question. On the one hand, it seems plausible to argue that the United States was satisfied with the prevailing arrangement of the international system. After all, the military, political, and economic position of the United States was essentially unchallenged at this time. Moreover, the behavior of the United States government is consistent with this interpretation of its preferences. For instance, a preference for the status quo over all other outcomes would explain the failure of the United States to intervene during the 1953 rioting in East Germany and it would also explain the Eisenhower administration's refusal to permit a full airing of a proposal that called for presenting the Soviets with a number of ultimatums demanding, inter alia, a revision of the de facto postwar division of Europe.[5]

On the other hand, however, given the ephemeral quality of the American position of dominance, it also seems reasonable to suggest, as Howard (1983) does, that the Eisenhower administration was not attached to the certain-to-deteriorate status quo. Indeed, the idea of launching a preventive strike did surface, albeit briefly, within the American bureaucracy, indicating that at least some strategic thinkers were dissatisfied with future power projections (Rosenberg 1983).

Are there any other interpretations of the deterrence model consistent with the assumption that a dominant United States was not self-deterred during this period? There are three. From tables 7.1 and 7.2, it can be seen that deterrence remains stable, even when American preponderance is assumed, as

5. In turn, Soviet actions surpressing these riots require the assumption that they (correctly) estimated that the United States would not involve itself in this conflict.

long as the retaliatory threat of the Soviet Union is credible. In other words, stable deterrence can also be explained but only if a Soviet preference to resist any attempt by the United States to impose a new order is postulated.

Is such an assumption tenable in the face of Soviet inferiority and vulnerability? Kahan (1975, 29) argues as much:

> It seems certain that moral factors kept U.S. leaders from entertaining the possibility of a preventive strike; such a move would have been antithetical to the traditional American policy of eschewing surprise attack. But practical considerations undoubtedly influenced the decision as well—a U.S. counterforce strike could not be assured of completely eliminating the USSR's capability to retaliate with nuclear weapons. Even if Soviet long-range delivery capabilities could be destroyed, the United States could not be confident of preventing the USSR from inflicting substantial damage on Western Europe with its medium-range force.

Curiously, Kahan's explanation for the absence of an American attack during the first Eisenhower administration (needlessly) confuses both of the explanations offered herein. If moral considerations in fact had an impact on the calculus of American decision-makers to reject a preemptive war when the United States enjoyed clear-cut military superiority, then the United States was self-deterred, that is, it preferred the status quo to attacking the Soviet Union, regardless of whether or not the Soviets retaliated. But if strategic considerations were paramount, then the absence of a first-strike capability, coupled with a capable and credible retaliatory threat of the Soviets (to attack Western Europe), can explain the (non)decision of the Eisenhower administration. Consequently, either of these explanations provides sufficient explanatory conditions; neither, though, is necessary.

While both of these explanations seem innocuous enough, there are some problematic implications associated with each of them. For instance, if Kahan's strategic explanation is accepted, then the possibility that a credible retaliatory threat is not necessarily a function of either inferiority or vulnerability must also be accepted since this assumption is necessary to account for systemic stability in a relationship of mutual deterrence.

Moreover, the classic realpolitik hypothesis that power imbalances are precursors to war is seemingly contradicted by either the moral or the strategic explanation for the stability of this period, since the system remained stable at a time of very obvious strategic inequality. It is *seemingly* contradicted only because the fundamental assumption associated with the present analysis, that is, that the United States was indeed preponderant, must be accepted for the balance-of-power hypothesis to be rejected.

Finally, if the balance-of-power model is to be salvaged, then the argument that conventional superiority can offset nuclear inferiority must also be accepted, since a balance of power can be said to have existed from 1951 to 1955 only if this possibility is admitted. A further implication of this argument is that nuclear weapons cannot be considered sui generis, as Brodie (1946) and other early deterrence theorists have suggested.[6] And if this extension is allowed, then the current United States deployment of intermediate-range ballistic missiles in Europe can also be questioned on strategic grounds.

7.4 The Period of Mutual Vulnerability: 1956–61

The third distinct period of the United States–Soviet Union strategic relationship covered, roughly, the years 1956 to 1961. During this period the American monopoly of strategic delivery vehicles was broken. In the now famous "flyby" of the long-range Bison bombers during the June 1955 Aviation Day show in Moscow, the Soviets apparently demonstrated the capability of repeated intercontinental strikes at American indus-

6. For empirical evidence suggesting that conventional superiority is more important than nuclear superiority, see Bueno de Mesquita (1981, 1985a), Kugler (1984), and Huth and Russett (1984).

trial and population centers. Moreover, even though it was later determined that the Soviets never invested heavily in the production of the Bison, the strategic importance of the growing number of medium-range Badger bombers was enhanced with the entry of thermonuclear weapons into the Soviet arsenal during this period. Since the vast destructive power of hydrogen bombs rendered implausible a war of attrition between the superpowers, the Soviet fleet of Badgers, capable of a one-way mission against the United States, now constituted a serious strategic threat (Quester 1970, 126–29). Suddenly, the United States was no longer invulnerable to a preemptive or a retaliatory nuclear strike by the Soviet Union.[7]

In this context, it is worth pointing out that the rapid development and deployment of intercontinental ballistic missiles by both superpowers toward the end of the decade reinforced, rather than precipitated, the distinguishing characteristics of the period of mutual vulnerability. Because the first-generation ICBMs used liquid fuel and were deployed in unhardened silos, each side remained vulnerable to a massive "spasm" attack by the other, although the precautionary measures taken by both superpowers probably precluded either one from attaining a first-strike capability. Thus, the acquisition of an intercontinental strike force by the Soviet Union induced a strategic stalemate characterized by each superpower suffering from what Schelling (1960) has called "the reciprocal fear of surprise attack."

It should not be surprising that, in a world in which each superpower was vulnerable to a thermonuclear strike by the other, many analysts started to question the meaning of the term strategic "superiority." Although the United States maintained a lead during this and the subsequent period in both the number of warheads and intercontinental delivery vehicles, the

---

7. There is a difference of opinion in the strategic literature about the ability of the Soviet Union to inflict significant damage on the United States during this period. (See, for example, Kugler 1984). If this argument is accepted, the conclusions of this section do not apply.

Soviet arsenal was such that William Kaufmann (1956, 21) could warn at the very beginning of this period that "if we are challenged to fulfill the threat of massive retaliation, we will be likely to suffer costs as great as those we inflict."

To their credit, theorists on both sides were aware of the subtleties of the evolving strategic environment. The Soviets, for instance, stopped talking about burying the West and instead stressed the importance of "peaceful coexistence." For its part, the Eisenhower administration, rather than attempt to maintain a position of strict numerical superiority, as counseled by the leadership of the American air force, moved to embrace the concept of strategic "adequacy" or "sufficiency" (Kahan 1975, 31). Under this doctrine, the United States would not need to maintain a quantitative edge over the Soviets in every conceivable category of nuclear weaponry. What was more important was the ability to inflict unacceptable damage on the Soviet Union in case of a superpower confrontation. As Secretary of the Air Force Donald Quarles put it, what mattered was not "the *relative* strength of the two opposed forces. It is the *absolute* power in the hands of each, and . . . the substantial invulnerability of this power to interdiction" (quoted in Kahan 1975, 33).

The implication was, of course, that neither side could expect to win a nuclear war. Thus technological advances had rendered obsolete Clausewitz's famous aphorism about the nature of warfare. Under conditions of mutual vulnerability, it became difficult to imagine a set of conditions under which the costs associated with fighting a war would even come close to being outweighed by the potential benefits of prevailing in such a confrontation. Brodie's (1946) early observation that the only purpose of nuclear weapons was to prevent war had finally become the reality.[8]

Needless to say, the altered environment had important stra-

8. In other words, the concept of holding power was no longer relevant since the war-of-attrition scenario associated with it was now clearly an idea whose time had passed.

tegic consequences. Whereas previously the Eisenhower administration could, and did, attempt to maintain the status quo by threatening transgressors with a nuclear attack, now such a threat against either the Soviet Union or its allies appeared to lack credibility. Since the execution of a nuclear threat also implied enormous costs for the United States, critics charged that the administration's "New Look" policy, which relied heavily on the nuclear threat of "massive retaliation," was now obsolete. Given the symmetry of the superpower relationship, what was true for the United States was also true for the Soviet Union. If the American nuclear threat lacked credibility, so did the Soviets'.

In the deterrence literature, the superpower relationship of this period increasingly came to be represented by the game of Chicken. The analogy was compelling. Recall that the outcome associated with mutual punishment in this game is the worst for both players. Perforce, in Chicken, both players lack a credible threat.

The analogy was also revealing. Even without a first-strike capability, deterrence is extremely unstable in *thermonuclear* Chicken. In this game, each player should have no compunction about moving away from the status quo in order to induce its best outcome, since the other player would not rationally punish the first by executing the threat; such an action would only terminate the game at the outcome that was worst for the aggrieved player (Achen 1986).

Chicken, then, represents in its starkest form the problem associated with mutual deterrence in the nuclear age. There are, however, two solutions to the instability problem inherent in this game. Interestingly, the first was pursued by the Eisenhower administration for as long as it remained in office; the second was implemented as American strategic policy by the Kennedy administration toward the end of the period of mutual vulnerability.

The policy pursued by the Eisenhower administration to preserve the status quo and maintain deterrence stability was to attempt to alter the structure of the game it played with the Soviets. Since the instability of the status quo in nuclear Chicken, and its unilateral deterrence analogue, can be directly traced to the absence of a credible threat, the Eisenhower administration sought to convince both the Soviets and its West European allies that it preferred nuclear war and its attendant costs to capitulating to a Soviet challenge. The task faced by the administration, and by its Soviet counterpart, then, was to make the irrational appear rational, the incredible, credible.

Such a stratagem was used with apparent success during the Berlin crisis of 1958–59 in which the Soviets had demanded an end to the Allied occupation of the divided city.[9] On several occasions Eisenhower suggested, not very subtly, that nuclear weapons would be used to defend Berlin. It is likely that the Soviets took these warnings seriously. In March 1959, Soviet premier Khrushchev withdrew his demand and accepted the administration's offer to discuss the Berlin issue within the context of a foreign ministers' conference (Kahan 1975, 26).

The Eisenhower strategy, in essence, was to deny that a problem existed and to act as if its threat was credible. Given the absence of a superpower war during this period, it is difficult to argue that this policy was not successful. To do so, one must postulate that *both* superpowers were satisfied status-quo players at this time. Otherwise, if the threat of nuclear retaliation is posited to be inherently incredible under conditions of strategic vulnerability, at least one player would have had an incentive to seek a significant readjustment of the existing order.

To ascribe a modicum of success to the Eisenhower administration's policy, however, is not to suggest that it was without flaws. As Quester (1970, 212) has pointed out, one problem with an almost total reliance on a nuclear deterrent was that the threat "might indeed be credible all around." Thus, in a setting

9. Snyder and Diesing (1977, 92–93) depict this crisis as a Prisoners' Dilemma game.

like Berlin, "where any military initiative had to fall to the
West rather than to the Soviet bloc," the Western leadership
might be presented with a very unpalatable choice: either nuclear war or capitulation. In other words, given mutually credible escalatory threats, each side would be deterred at the strategic level but, somewhat paradoxically, would not be deterred
from seeking unilateral advantages at the margin.

A burning strategic issue at the time, therefore, was whether
such untoward actions could be prevented. Stated differently,
would the strategic arsenals of the superpowers offset one another but still encourage each nation to probe the limits of the
other's resolve in a number of crises until the laws of probability caught up with them? Put still another way, how could
the status quo be stabilized in both the Chicken game played at
the substrategic level and in the Prisoners' Dilemma game
played on the strategic plane?

The answer to this question can be found in table 7.1. Deterrence is stable in Chicken as long as both players have the
ability to pass through mutual punishment by fighting a limited
war. Whether or not two nuclear powers could engage in such a
conflict without eventual escalation to a general war was, of
course, a hotly debated question during the late 1950s and the
early 1960s (Freedman 1981, chaps. 7 and 8). But the fact that
this particular question should arise at this particular time is
not at all surprising given the deductions of the deterrence
model developed herein.

At any rate, consistent with the deductions of this model,
critics of the New Look policy called for the development of
nonnuclear choices in order to deter the anticipated "salami
tactics" of the Soviets. While the Eisenhower administration
rejected this advice, the Kennedy administration did not. With
the transfer of power to the Democrats in 1961, the New Look
policy was replaced by the doctrine of "flexible response."
According to Kahan 1975, 76), "the key objective of flexible
response was to maintain forces capable of meeting conventional threats so that the United States would not be faced with

the choice of either using nuclear weapons or forgoing vital interests abroad because it lacked nonnuclear options."

The difference between these two approaches to deterrence can be seen by examining the actions taken by the Kennedy administration during its own Berlin crisis. When Khrushchev revived his demands for an end to the Allied occupation of the city at the Vienna summit meeting in June 1961, Kennedy's response was largely a conventional one: the National Guard was mobilized, 40,000 American troops were transferred to Europe, and Congress was asked to provide nearly $3 billion for increased defense spending. The reason for all of this is clear. As Quester (1970, 214) has astutely observed, if "the Russians were again molding the contest for Berlin into a game of 'chicken,' . . . [then] . . . the buildup of NATO forces, however widely advertised as changing the game, may in fact have amounted to the West's playing it."

7.5 The Second Period of American Superiority: 1962–66

An American strategic buildup, reluctantly agreed to by President Eisenhower and accelerated by President Kennedy, had by 1962 precipitated yet another distinct period in the superpower relationship. By most accounts, during the early 1960s the United States enjoyed an overwhelming margin of strategic superiority over the Soviet Union. This lead was in fact so large that the Soviet strategic force was vulnerable to an American first strike (Quester 1970, 216; Friedberg 1982, 69). Moreover, since the American augmentation included both Minuteman missiles in hardened underground silos and several Polaris submarines, the American strategic arsenal was invulnerable to preemptive action by the Soviets.

The transition to the second period of American strategic superiority was sudden and, to some extent, unanticipated. After demonstrating an ICBM capability in 1957 by launching Sputnik, the first earth-satellite, the Soviets decided not to invest heavily in their first-generation strategic missiles. But the Soviets apparently experienced some technical difficulties in developing their second-generation missiles. Thus, when coupled with the lag in Soviet deployment, the American strategic buildup resulted in a very asymmetric strategic situation.

There are only two interpretations of the deterrence model consistent with both the American first-strike capability and the absence of a superpower war at this time [games 64(48) and 76(72)]. Both of these interpretations posit the United States as a status-quo power with a credible retaliatory threat (see table 3.1.) Each of these conditions, therefore, is necessary to explain the observed stability of this period. Neither condition, though, by itself, is sufficient. Thus, even under conditions of preponderance, stability requires a credible deterrent threat.

At the strategic level it is difficult to argue that the American deterrent was not credible. After all, given the limited number of missiles in the Soviet arsenal, the United States would have had little to lose by *responding* to a Soviet attack. Nevertheless, as the Democrats themselves had pointed out in the 1960 presidential campaign, the credibility of such a threat still remained problematic in situations of "immediate" deterrence (Morgan 1983) at the substrategic level.

The significance afforded the distinction between the two levels of deterrence by the Kennedy administration was evident during the Cuban missile crisis of 1962. Even though American strategic power was at its zenith, and even though the missiles posed a direct threat to some parts of the United States, the administration felt compelled to respond to the Soviet initiative at the conventional level first. Thus, the blockade was hailed because it both communicated American resolve and because it left the Soviets with the unpalatable choice of backing down or escalating.

It is important to point out, however, that American tactics during the missile crisis were not completely conventional. As had been the case during the 1961 Berlin crisis, President

Kennedy was not reluctant to rattle his nuclear sabers, promising on one occasion "full nuclear retaliation" against the Soviet Union. Thus, while it is true that the United States enjoyed conventional superiority in the Caribbean, it does not follow that conventional dominance alone determined the outcome of this crisis. Indeed, one might question instead whether, given the stakes involved, a conventional response was redundant or even unnecessarily risky since a local incident could have, willy-nilly, sparked a wider exchange.

Whatever the case, though, the Kennedy administration had to play the game differently in the European theater. Despite the fact that Western forces were increased on the Continent after 1961, the Soviets continued to have the upper hand. Could not, then, the Soviets play the same way the United States had in Cuba by presenting the United States with the same hard choice between accepting an attempted fait accompli and precipitating a general war?

It was this fear that led American decision-makers to enunciate the doctrine of a "counterforce strategy." In contrast to the doctrine of massive retaliation, which the Democrats had publicly denigrated, the idea of a counterforce strategy discriminated among potential targets in a nuclear conflict. Instead of visualizing a single spasm-attack on Soviet society, a counterforce attack or controlled response would focus only on Soviet military targets. Such a "no cities" doctrine, it was felt, would enhance the credibility of the American deterrent since it would not involve the indiscriminate destruction of civilians. Given the vulnerability of Soviet strategic forces at the time, and the American first-strike capability, such a strategy seemed reasonable.

7.6 The Period of Essential Equivalence: 1967 to date

The strategy seemed less reasonable, or at least eminently debatable, as the second period of American supremacy evolved into the last, and current, period of the superpower relationship.[10] After being "humiliated" and forced to back down during the 1962 missile crisis, the Soviet leadership decided to take the steps necessary to redress the strategic imbalance. The resultant buildup, which was further accelerated by Khrushchev's successors after 1964, was slower than the American buildup from 1960 to 1962, but it was impressive nonetheless. As late as 1964 the Soviet strategic force had been outnumbered by approximately a four-to-one ratio. But by the end of 1967 the Soviets were approaching parity with the United States. Under these circumstances the Johnson administration, understandably, lost some of its interest in counterforce strategies and instead shifted its defense policy in the direction of the doctrine of assured destruction. And when the Nixon administration took office in 1969, the notion of strategic "sufficiency" was resurrected to take account of the new reality.

Since 1967 the configuration of both the American and Soviet arsenals has undergone considerable change. But notwithstanding the development and deployment of MIRVs, more accurate ICBMs, larger and longer-range SSBNs, and the musings of some strategic thinkers, from 1967 to date neither side has had the capability to eliminate the other's ability to retaliate in kind in the event of a nuclear first strike. Since each side has enjoyed an invulnerable second-strike capability, the post-1967 era might be viewed as the "golden age of deterrence." In terms of Intriligator and Brito's model (1984), the superpower relationship of this period has been firmly ensconced in the "cone of mutual deterrence." [11]

Even still, stable deterrence cannot be said to be only a function of the MAD relationship. Needless to say, since the act of war involves human choice, the assurance of destruction depends upon the perception of each side that the other would

10. Some analyses date the beginning of this period much later. See, for example Kugler and Zagare (1986).

11. This is not to suggest that future technologies will be incapable of disturbing this relationship.

indeed retaliate if the status quo were transgressed. Thus, the rather facile conclusion is that either both sides did not need to be deterred since 1967, or that at least one side has maintained a credible threat in spite of the fact that execution of the threat implied the destruction of its own society.

Some important policy expectations, however, follow from this rather obvious observation. If stability depends upon one or both states establishing a credible threat, then it would not only be prudent, but one would also predict, that each super-power would go to considerable length to (1) assure the other that it intended to cooperate as long as the other also cooperated, and (2) that it would not accept a precipitous action by the other. In other words, tit-for-tat strategies are not only optimal but necessary for systemic stability. On the other hand, if each player lacked a credible threat (and the game was indeed Chicken), then one would expect that each side would race to preempt the other by making an "irrevocable commitment" to its non-status-quo strategy.

Much of the diplomatic record of this period can be more easily understood if the importance of establishing credibility is kept in mind. As has been seen, in both the 1967 and 1973 crises in the Middle East, each side made a considerable effort to make sure that the other understood that it would not tolerate any action by the other, or the other's allies, that would significantly erode its interests in the area. The worldwide alert of American strategic forces during the 1973 crisis was merely the most obvious of these actions. On the other hand, on both occasions, since it was Israel that was dominant in the local war, the United States also made every effort to assure the Soviets that it would not permit Israel to compromise either Syrian or Egyptian sovereignty.

The American commitment to South Vietnam until 1973 also seems much more understandable when viewed from this perspective. Even though United States decision-makers realized as early as 1968 that a military victory in Vietnam was not possible (Kissinger 1969), the American disengagement from this costly war was predicated upon a "peace with honor," so that American allies would not come to believe that the United States had "chickened out." [12]

7.7 Summary and Conclusions

In this chapter I have divided the strategic relationship of the United States and the Soviet Union into five distinct periods. These periods have been defined by the shifting strategic capabilities of the two superpowers. Three of these have been posited to be periods of overall strategic equivalence and two to be periods of American strategic superiority. Since each of the five periods differs from the others in some way, they can be viewed as historical controls that permit the impact of some of the most salient characteristics of a nuclear relationship to be explored.

Upon examination it is interesting to note that there is no one correct theoretically based explanation for the stability of the postwar period. In general, a number of logically consistent and empirically plausible configurations of player preferences exist for each of the five periods that can be used to explain the absence of a superpower war. Moreover, although these possible explanations contracted in number as the superpower relationship developed, there are only two explanations that are consistently present throughout the entire superpower relationship. The first is the rather innocuous explanation that both actors have been satisfied status-quo powers since 1945. The second posits the United States as a status-quo power in a unilateral deterrence game with the Soviet Union. It is worth mentioning that for one of the five distinct periods, i.e., 1962–66, this latter explanation is the only explanation of strategic stability consistent with the nature of the superpower relationship.

To sustain this latter argument for the entire postwar period,

12. See Zagare (1977) for a game-theoretic analysis of the Vietnam conflict.

though, one of several emendations is necessary for the years 1948 to 1950. First, one could assume that the Soviet Union was also a status-quo power for these years, or that Soviet leaders were risk-averse at the time, or that the United States was perceived to be more powerful and was thought to be able to successfully wage a war-of-attrition against the Soviet Union. While the last of these assumptions might be debated, the first two are without strong empirical support.

It is not necessary, of course, to hold that states exhibit consistent preference schedules over time. Leaders and regimes come and go, and with them fundamental orientations and perceptual predispositions can be expected to change. Yet theories pitched at the level of the nation-state that posit uniform and eternal goals for nations often ignore this simple fact.

Even though a number of rational-choice explanations exist for the stability of the superpower relationship since 1945, several interpretations of the motivations of the two superpowers can be eliminated since they are not consistent with the empirical record. For instance, one cannot hold that the United States had a first-strike capability in the early 1960s without also accepting the position that the United States was a status-quo power at the time. Also, one cannot argue, as does Howard (1983) that the United States was not a status-quo power from 1951 to 1955 without also claiming that at a time of very obvious strategic inferiority the Soviet deterrent was both capable and credible. While this may in fact been the case, then it also follows that the capability requirements for successful deterrence are much lower than are generally supposed.

Similarly, Achen's (1986) argument that the costs of carrying out a deterrent threat are perceived to far outweigh evaluations of the costs that would accrue should the status quo be violated can be rejected on empirical grounds, at least for the current period. As Achen himself points out, deterrence is unstable, and peace is irrational, when this argument is accepted.[13]

13. As indicated in chapter 1, Brams and Kilgour's (1985a, 1985c) model also does not resolve the paradox. As with Achen's charge against deterrence theory in gen-

One may, of course, view this as a paradox of deterrence as does Achen. But seen from another perspective, it is quite revealing about the nature of preferences at the leadership level. Statesmen seem to prefer, or at least are perceived to prefer, to be "better dead than red" or, alternatively, "better a grave than a capitalist wage slave." The Jews at Masada have not been the only ones to reveal their preferences for a good that transcends life itself. Unfortunately, while credible, their threat was not capable to deter their enemies.

From this it follows that the fear in some quarters of the strategic community that one side or the other (i.e., the Soviets) might be tempted to eliminate the increasingly vulnerable land-based missile force of the other (i.e., the United States) seems unfounded. If the superpowers are able to make credible their threat to retaliate, and it appears that they have, then stability will follow as long as an invulnerable second-strike capability is maintained.

This also suggests that the key to successful deterrence resides at the level of individual decision-makers whose preference projections and perceptions define the nature of the deterrence relationship. Successful deterrence cannot, therefore, be ensured simply by building more and more missiles and praying that an accident does not occur (Intriligator and Brito 1984). Seemingly reasonable leaders who dwell upon the costs of nuclear war are likely to undermine the credibility of its nation's threat and, consequently, deterrence stability itself, whatever the objective environment may be like. Conversely, as Kugler and Zagare (1986) point out, leaders who appear to be risk-acceptant may even precipitate preemption by the other side. Deterrence, then, is fundamentally a psychological relationship. As such, it is extremely fragile.

---

eral, their model rests upon the supposition that each player is simultaneously rational (in deciding whether or not to attack) and irrational (in deciding whether or not to retaliate).

Epilogue

In the preceding pages, I have used the theory of moves to develop a model of the deterrence relationship. In my opinion, this framework has proven to be an extremely potent device for analyzing deterrence and for generating insights into its dynamics. In what follows, I will briefly highlight the most important conclusions associated with this model. It is important to keep in mind, however, that if some of these results seem obvious, they are obvious only because they have been deduced from a small set of reasonable assumptions about the calculus of deterrence. They are *not* ad hoc propositions but rather constitute a set of interrelated hypotheses about the nature of this relationship. Almost without exception, similar or contrary hypotheses can be pointed to in the strategic literature. What distinguishes these findings from the free-floating propositions is the fact that those reported below are grounded in a theoretical framework that provides both logical consistency and a firm explanatory base.

Capability emerges from this study as the sine qua non of deterrence. It is an absolutely necessary ingredient of the deterrence equation. Without it, deterrence of a revisionist player will always fail. Still, a capable retaliatory threat is not a sufficient condition for deterrence success. Under certain conditions, even when both players are able to hurt one another, deterrence is not stable.

Credibility is not quite the magic ingredient that it is claimed to be, but it remains a very important part of the deterrence relationship nonetheless. Credibility is neither a necessary nor a sufficient condition for successful deterrence. Without a capable threat, a player whose threat is credible will still be unable to deter an opponent who prefers to upset the status quo. And, under some conditions, deterrence may constitute a stable relationship, even when each player's threat lacks inherent credibility.

Like credibility, a power advantage is neither necessary nor sufficient for deterrence to work. A weaker player with a capable and credible threat, for instance, should be able to deter a stronger opponent. Conversely, a dominant power may, under certain conditions, be unable to deter its weaker adversary. Thus, at the theoretical level at least, deterrence stability is not a direct consequence of either a balance or an imbalance of power.

All of which suggests that deterrence interactions are intricate and unusually complex. There is no one-to-one relationship between any single dimension of the model and overall deterrence stability. Slight alterations in one or another parameter, such as the nature of each player's retaliatory threat, power, offensive ability, weapons characteristics, and attitude toward risk may have dramatic consequences for the success, or the failure, of deterrence.

Another interesting insight that emerges from the theoretical development of the model—and is supported in its application—concerns the incentive that players in deterrence games have to try to create or reinforce interactions that share the structure of game theory's notorious Prisoners' Dilemma game. As we saw in the analysis of both the 1967 and the 1973 crises in the Middle East, as well as in the examination of the superpower strategic relationship, decision-makers have a tendency to respond to crisis situations by conveying tit-for-tat communications to one another, conveying a willingness to compromise but also a determination to respond to the untoward behavior of the other. Not only does the structure of this game, then, describe the conditions conducive to stable mutual deterrence, but it also explains the obvious and well-documented discrepancies between the behavior exhibited by states during actual crisis situations and some of the more esoteric crisis-management strategies suggested by some deterrence theorists (Young 1968; Snyder and Diesing 1977).

The stability characteristics of the status quo in the prototypical deterrence game are also suggestive of another salient characteristic of these relationships. Deterrence constitutes a stable relationship in a Prisoners' Dilemma game, but only when the compromise outcome is the status quo and both players have the ability to punish departures from it. Moreover, the deterrence equilibrium in this game, while retentive, is not an attractive equilibrium. This means that even a temporary disruption of this equilibrium implies the rupture of deterrence. Thus, even in its ideal manifestation, deterrence is rickety and fragile.

The delicate balance of terror is underscored by the analysis of the strategic relationship of the United States and the Soviet Union. Fortunately, this relationship has remained stable despite the fact that it has undergone considerable evolution since its inception in 1945. Some may interpret the continuing stability of this relationship as evidence of the robustness of deterrence. But there is more here than meets the eye. It appears that deterrence is not directly a function of those variables that are most easily manipulated by decision-makers, that is, the nature and composition of each side's strategic arsenal. Rather deterrence stability resides "in the heads" of world leaders. It depends not only on obvious objective factors but may also hinge on the perceptions, or misperceptions, of those who have the ability to induce Armageddon. Such factors, unlike the balance of military power, can be subject to quick and erratic changes, as coups d'état, revolutions, elections, illness, and other forces bring about fundamental leadership changes. Deterrence is indeed a tenuous relationship.

In a sense, then, this analysis has bittersweet implications.

Deterrence works, or seems to work, more often than not. Despite some obvious exceptions, the world is generally peaceful, at least when measured by the possibilities. Yet, in the nuclear age, this is hardly reassuring.

Given the fragile nature of this relationship, one is naturally led to ask if there is a better way to manage world affairs. I have no magic elixir to offer here. Perhaps, some day, other approaches to international relations will render unnecessary such a ghastly approach to the world about us, provided that deterrence can deliver us to the millennium. Until then, however, we surely remain "prisoners" of our own imagination.

References

Achen, Christopher H. 1986. "A Darwinian View of Deterrence." In Jacek Kugler and Frank C. Zagare, eds., *The Stability of Deterrence*. Monograph Series in World Affairs. Denver: University of Denver School of International Studies.

Allison, Graham T., and Frederic A. Morris. 1976. "Armaments and Arms Control: Exploring the Determinants of Military Weapons." In Franklin A. Long and George W. Rathjens, eds., *Arms, Defense Policy, and Arms Control*. New York: W. W. Norton.

Arrow, Kenneth J. 1951. *Social Choice and Individual Values*. New Haven: Yale University Press.

Axelrod, Robert. 1984. *The Evolution of Cooperation*. New York: Basic Books.

Bar-Zohar, Michael. 1970. *Embassies in Crisis: Diplomats and Demagogues Behind the Six-Day War*. Englewood-Cliffs, N.J.: Prentice-Hall.

Baugh, William H. 1984. *The Politics of Nuclear Balance*. New York: Longman.

Baylis, John, Ken Booth, John Garnett, and Phil Williams. 1975. *Contemporary Strategy: Theories and Policies*. New York: Holmes & Meier.

Blechman, Barry M., and Douglas M. Hart. 1982. "The Political Utility of Nuclear Weapons: The 1973 Middle East Crisis." *International Security* 7: 132–56.

Brams, Steven J. 1975. *Game Theory and Politics*. New York: The Free Press.

———. 1976. *Paradoxes in Politics*. New York: The Free Press.

———. 1977. "Deception in 2 × 2 Games." *Journal of Peace Science* 2: 171–203.

———. 1983. *Superior Beings: If They Exist, How Would We Know?* New York: Springer-Verlag.

————. 1985. *Superpower Games: Applying Game Theory to Superpower Conflict.* New Haven: Yale University Press.

Brams, Steven J., and Marek P. Hessel. 1982. "Absorbing Outcomes in 2 × 2 Games." *Behavioral Science* 27: 393–401.

————. 1983. "Staying Power in Sequential Games." *Theory and Decision* 15: 279–302.

————. 1984. "Threat Power in Sequential Games." *International Studies Quarterly* 28: 23–44.

Brams, Steven J., and D. Marc Kilgour. 1985a. "Optimal Deterrence." *Social Philosophy and Policy* 31: 118–35.

————. 1985b. "Rational Deescalation." Mimeographed.

————. 1985c. "The Path to Stable Deterrence." In Urs Luterbacher and Michael D. Ward, eds., *Dynamic Models of International Conflict.* Boulder, Colo.: Lynne Rienner Publishers.

Brams, Steven J., and Donald Wittman. 1981. "Nonmyopic Equilibria in 2 × 2 Games." *Conflict Management and Peace Science* 6: 39–62.

Brams, Steven J., and Frank C. Zagare. 1977. "Deception in Simple Voting Games." *Social Science Research* 6: 257–72.

————. 1981. "Double Deception: Two Against One in Three-Person Games." *Theory and Decision* 13: 81–90.

Brecher, Michael. 1975. *Decisions in Israel's Foreign Policy.* New Haven: Yale University Press.

Brodie, Bernard, ed. 1946. *The Absolute Weapon: Atomic Power and World Order.* New York: Harcourt Brace.

Brodie, Bernard. 1959. "The Anatomy of Deterrence." *World Politics* 11: 173–79.

Bueno de Mesquita, Bruce. 1981. *The War Trap.* New Haven: Yale University Press.

————. 1985a. "The War Trap Revisited." *The American Political Science Review* 79: 156–77.

————. 1985b. Personal communication, February 15.

Bueno de Mesquita, Bruce, and William H. Riker. 1982. "An Assessment of the Merits of Selective Nuclear Proliferation." *Journal of Conflict Resolution* 26: 283–306.

Bull, Hedley. 1961. *The Control of the Arms Race: Disarmament and Arms Control in the Missile Age.* New York: Praeger.

Colman, Andrew. 1982. *Game Theory and Experimental Games: The Study of Strategic Interaction.* Oxford: Pergamon Press.

Crawford, Vincent P. 1985. "Dynamic Games and Dynamic Contract Theory." *Journal of Conflict Resolution* 29: 195–224.

Davison, W. Phillips. 1958. *The Berlin Blockade: A Study in Cold War Politics*. Princeton: Princeton University Press.

Dayan, Moshe. 1976. *Moshe Dayan: Story of My Life*. New York: William Morrow.

Department of State Bulletin. October 27, 1973.

Deutsch, Karl W. 1978. *The Analysis of International Relations*. 2d ed. Englewood-Cliffs, N.J.: Prentice-Hall.

Ellsberg, Daniel. 1959. "The Theory and Practice of Blackmail." Lecture at the Lowell Institute, Boston, Mass., March 10. Reprinted in Oran R. Young, ed., *Bargaining; Formal Theories of Negotiation*. Urbana: University of Illinois Press, 1975.

———. 1961. "The Crude Analysis of Strategic Choice." *American Economic Review* 51: 472–78.

Fiorina, Morris P., and Kenneth A. Shepsle. 1982. "Equilibrium Disequilibrium, and the General Possibility of a Science of Politics." In Peter C. Ordeshook and Kenneth A. Shepsle, eds., *Political Equilibrium*. Boston: Kluwer-Nijhoff.

Fraser, Niall M., and Keith Hipel. 1979. "Solving Complex Conflicts." *IEEE Transactions on Systems, Man, and Cybernetics*, SCM-9, 12: 805–16.

Freedman, Lawrence. 1981. *The Evolution of Nuclear Strategy*. New York: St. Martin's Press.

Friedberg, Aaron L. 1982. "The Evolution of U.S. Strategic 'Doctrine'—1945 to 1981." In Samuel P. Huntington, ed., *The Strategic Imperative: New Policies for American Security*. Cambridge: Ballinger.

Gaddis, John Lewis. 1982. *Strategies of Containment*. Oxford: Oxford University Press.

Garnett, John. 1975. "Strategic Studies and Its Assumptions." In John Baylis, Ken Booth, John Garnett, and Phil Williams, eds., *Contemporary Strategy: Theories and Policies*. New York: Holmes & Meier.

George, Alexander L., and Richard Smoke. 1974. *Deterrence in American Foreign Policy*. New York: Columbia University Press.

Glassman, Jon D. 1975. *Arms for the Arabs: The Soviet Union and War in the Middle East*. Baltimore: The Johns Hopkins University Press.

Goldblat, Jozef, and Victor Millán. 1983. *The Falklands/Malvinas Conflict: A Spur to Arms Build-Ups.* Stockholm: SIPRI.

Guetzkow, Harold. 1982. "Review of *The War Trap.*" *The Review of Politics* 44: 626–28.

Haig, Alexander M. 1984. *Caveat: Realism, Reagan and Foreign Policy.* New York: Macmillan.

Hardin, Russell. 1971. "Collective Action as an Agreeable n-Prisoners' Dilemma." *Behavioral Science* 16: 472–81.

Henderson, John M. and Richard E. Quandt. 1971. *Microeconomic Theory.* 2d ed. New York: McGraw-Hill.

Hirshleifer, Jack. 1985. "Protocol, Payoff, and Equilibrium: Game Theory and Social Modelling." Mimeographed.

Holsti, Ole R., Richard A. Brody, and Robert C. North. 1964. "Measuring Affect and Action in International Relations Models: Empirical Materials from the 1962 Cuban Crisis." *Journal of Peace Research* 1: 170–89.

Hopkins, Raymond F., and Richard W. Mansbach. 1973. *Structure and Process in International Politics.* New York: Harper and Row.

Howard, Michael. 1983. *The Causes of War.* Cambridge: Harvard University Press.

Howard, Nigel. 1971. *Paradoxes of Rationality: Theory of Metagames and Political Behavior.* Cambridge: MIT Press.

Huth, Paul, and Bruce Russett. 1984. "What Makes Deterrence Work?" *World Politics* 36: 496–526.

Intriligator, Michael D., and Dagobert L. Brito. 1984. "Can Arms Races Lead to the Outbreak of War?" *Journal of Conflict Resolution* 28: 63–84.

Jervis, Robert. 1979. "Deterrence Theory Revisited." *World Politics* 31: 289–324.

Johnson, Lyndon Baines. 1971. *The Vantage Point.* New York: Holt, Rinehart & Winston.

Kahan, Jerome H. 1975. *Security in the Nuclear Age.* Washington, D.C.: The Brookings Institution.

Kahn, Herman. 1960. *On Thermonuclear War.* Princeton: Princeton University Press.

———. 1962. *Thinking about the Unthinkable.* New York: Horizon Press.

———. 1965. *On Escalation.* New York: Praeger.

Kalb, Marvin, and Bernard Kalb. 1974. *Kissinger*. Boston: Little, Brown.

Kaplan, Fred. 1983. *The Wizards of Armageddon*. New York: Simon and Schuster.

Kaplan, Morton A. 1958. "The Calculus of Nuclear Deterrence." *World Politics* 11: 20–43.

Kaufmann, William. 1956. "The Requirements of Deterrence." In William Kaufmann, ed., *Military Policy and National Security*. Princeton: Princeton University Press.

Kavka, Gregory S. 1980. "Deterrence, Utility, and Rational Choice." *Theory and Decision* 12: 41–60.

———. 1982. "Deterrence and Utility Again: A Response to Bernard." *Theory and Decision* 14: 99–102.

Kennan, George F. 1967. *Memoirs: 1925–1950*. Boston: Little, Brown.

Khouri, Fred J. 1968. *The Arab-Israeli Dilemma*. New York: Syracuse University Press.

Kilgour, D. Marc. 1984. "Equilibria for Far-Sighted Players." *Theory and Decision* 16: 135–57.

———. 1985. "Anticipation and Stability in Two-Person Non-Cooperative Games." In Urs Luterbacher and Michael D. Ward, eds., *Dynamic Models of International Conflict*. Boulder, Colo.: Lynne Rienner Publishers.

Kilgour, D. Marc, and Frank C. Zagare. 1985. "Holding Power in Sequential Games." Mimeographed.

Kissinger, Henry A. 1969. "The Vietnam Negotiations." *Foreign Affairs* 47: 211–34.

———. 1982. *Years of Upheaval*. Boston: Little, Brown.

Kugler, Jacek. 1984. "Terror without Deterrence." *Journal of Conflict Resolution* 28: 470–506.

Kugler, Jacek, and Frank C. Zagare. 1986. "Risk, Deterrence, and War." In Jacek Kugler and Frank C. Zagare, eds., *The Stability of Deterrence*. Monograph Series in World Affairs. Denver: University of Denver Graduate School of International Studies.

Laquer, Walter. 1974. *Confrontation: The Middle East and World Politics*. New York: Quadrangle Books.

Luce, R. Duncan, and Howard Raiffa. 1957. *Games and Decisions: Introduction and Critical Survey*. New York: John Wiley & Sons.

MacIntyre, Alasdair. 1973. "The Essential Contestability of Some Social Concepts." *Ethics* 84: 1–9.

Manchester, William. 1973. *The Glory and the Dream: A Narrative History of America: 1932–1972.* 2 vols. Boston: Little, Brown.

Morgan, Patrick M. 1983. *Deterrence: A Conceptual Analysis.* 2d ed. Beverly Hills, Calif.: Sage.

Morgenstern, Oskar. 1959. *The Question of National Defense.* New York: Random House.

———. 1961. "Review of The *Strategy of Conflict.*" *Southern Economic Journal,* 28: 105.

Muzzio, Douglas. 1982. *Watergate Games: Strategies, Choices, Outcomes.* New York: New York University Press.

Nash, John. 1951. "Non-cooperative Games." *Annals of Mathematics* 54: 286–95.

Nixon, Richard M. 1978. *RN: The Memoirs of Richard Nixon.* New York: Grosset & Dunlap.

Ordeshook, Peter C. 1980. "Political Disequilibrium and Scientific Inquiry: A Comment on William Riker's 'Implications from the Disequilibrium of Majority Rule for the Study of Institutions." *American Political Science Review* 74: 447–50.

Organski, A. F. K., and Jacek Kugler. 1980. *The War Ledger.* Chicago: University of Chicago Press.

Perlmutter, Amos. 1978. *Politics and the Military in Israel, 1967–1977.* London: Frank Cass.

Quandt, William B. 1977. *Decade of Decisions: American Foreign Policy Toward the Arab-Israeli Conflict, 1967–1976.* Berkeley: University of California Press.

Quester, George H. 1970. *Nuclear Diplomacy.* New York: Dunellen.

———. 1982. "Six Causes of War." *The Jerusalem Journal of International Relations* 6: 1–23.

Rapoport, Anatol. 1964. *Strategy and Conscience.* New York: Harper and Row.

———. 1966. *Two-Person Game Theory: The Essential Ideas.* Ann Arbor: University of Michigan Press.

Rapoport, Anatol, and Melvin Guyer. 1966. "A Taxonomy of 2 × 2 Games." *General Systems: Yearbook of the Society for General Systems Research* 11: 203–14.

Rapoport, Anatol, Melvin J. Guyer, and David G. Gordon. 1976. *The 2 × 2 Game.* Ann Arbor: University of Michigan Press.

Reston, James. 1973a. "The Hidden Compromise." *New York Times.*
October 19: 43.

———. 1973b. "A Crisis a Day." *New York Times.* October 26: 43.

Riker, William H., and Peter C. Ordeshook. 1973. *An Introduction to Positive Political Theory.* Englewood-Cliffs, N.J.: Prentice-Hall.

Rosenau, James N. 1967. "The Premises and Promises of Decision-Making Analysis." In James C. Charlesworth, ed., *Contemporary Political Analysis.* New York: The Free Press.

Rosenberg, David Alan. 1983. "The Origins of Overkill: Nuclear Weapons and American Strategy, 1945–1960." *International Security* 7: 3–69.

Rubinstein, Alvin Z. 1977. Red Star on the Nile: The Soviet-Egyptian Influence Relationship since the June War. Princeton: Princeton University Press.

Russett, Bruce. 1983. *The Prisoners of Insecurity.* San Francisco: W. H. Freeman.

Safran, Nadav. 1969. *From War to War: The Arab-Israeli Confrontation, 1948–1967.* New York: Pegasus.

Schelling, Thomas C. 1960. *The Strategy of Conflict.* Cambridge: Harvard University Press.

———. 1966. *Arms and Influence.* New Haven: Yale University Press.

Schoemaker, Paul J. H. 1982. "The Expected Utility Model: Its Variants, Purposes, Evidence and Limitations." *Journal of Economic Literature* 20: 529–63.

Schotter, Andrew, and Gerhard Schwödiauer. 1980. "Economics and the Theory of Games: A Survey." *Journal of Economic Literature* 18: 479–527.

Shubik, Martin. 1982. *Game Theory and the Social Sciences: Concepts and Solutions.* Cambridge: MIT Press.

Smith, Theresa C. 1982. *Trojan Peace: Some Deterrence Propositions Tested.* Monograph Series in World Affairs. Denver: University of Denver Graduate School of International Studies.

Smoke, Richard. 1984. *National Security and the Nuclear Dilemma.* Reading, Mass.: Addison-Wesley.

Snyder, Glenn H. 1961. *Deterrence and Defense: Toward A Theory of National Security.* Princeton: Princeton University Press.

———. 1972. "Crisis Bargaining." In Charles F. Hermann, ed.,

International Crises: Insights from Behavioral Research. New York: The Free Press.

Snyder, Glenn H., and Paul Diesing. 1977. *Conflict Among Nations: Bargaining, Decision Making and System Structure in International Crises.* Princeton: Princeton University Press.

Stein, Arthur A. 1982. "When Misperception Matters." *World Politics* 34: 505–26.

Triska, Jan F., and David D. Finley. 1968. *Soviet Foreign Policy.* New York: Macmillan.

Verba, Sidney. 1961. "Assumptions of Rationality and Non-rationality in Models of the International System." In Klaus Knorr and Sidney Verba, eds., *The International System: Theoretical Essays.* Princeton: Princeton University Press.

Wagner, Abraham R. 1974. *Crisis Decision-Making: Israel's Experience in 1967 and 1973.* New York: Praeger.

Wagner, R. Harrison. 1982. "Deterrence and Bargaining." *Journal of Conflict Resolution* 26: 329–58.

———. 1983. "The Theory of Games and the Problem of International Cooperation." *American Political Science Review* 77: 330–46.

———. 1984. "The Theory of Games and the Balance of Power." Paper delivered at the Annual Meeting of the American Political Science Association, Washington, D.C., August 30–September 2.

Walker, Stephen G. 1977. "The Interface Between Beliefs and Behavior: Henry Kissinger's Operational Code and the Vietnam War." *Journal of Conflict Resolution* 21: 129–68.

Williams, Phil. 1975. "Crisis Management." In John Baylis, Ken Booth, John Garnett, and Phil Williams, eds., *Contemporary Strategy: Theories and Policies.* New York: Holmes & Meier.

Wittman, Donald. 1979. "How a War Ends: A Rational Model Approach." *Journal of Conflict Resolution* 23: 743–63.

Wohlstetter, Albert. 1974a. "Is There a Strategic Arms Race?" *Foreign Policy* 15: 3–20.

———. 1974b. "Rivals, But No 'Race'." *Foreign Policy* 16: 48–81.

Young, Oran R. 1968. *The Politics of Force: Bargaining During International Crises.* Princeton: Princeton University Press.

Young, Oran R., ed. 1975. *Bargaining: Formal Theories of Negotiations.* Urbana: University of Illinois Press.

Zagare, Frank C. 1977. "A Game-Theoretic Analysis of the Vietnam Negotiations: Preferences and Strategies, 1968–1973." *Journal of Conflict Resolution* 21: 663–84.

———. 1979. "The Geneva Conference of 1954: A Case of Tacit Deception." *International Studies Quarterly* 23: 390–411.

———. 1981. "Nonmyopic Equilibria and the Middle East Crisis of 1967." *Conflict Management and Peace Science* 5: 139–62.

———. 1982a. "Competing Game-Theoretic Explanations: The Geneva Conference of 1954." *International Studies Quarterly* 26: 141–47.

———. 1982b. "Review of *The War Trap*." *American Political Science Review* 76: 738–39.

———. 1983. "A Game-Theoretic Evaluation of the 1973 Cease-Fire Alert Decision." *Journal of Peace Research* 20: 73–86.

———. 1984a. *Game Theory: Concepts and Applications*. Beverly Hills, Calif.: Sage Publications.

———. 1984b. "Limited-Move Equilibria in 2 × 2 Games." *Theory and Decision* 16: 1–19.

———. 1985a. "The Pathologies of Unilateral Deterrence." In Urs Luterbacher and Michael D. Ward, eds., *Dynamic Models of International Conflict*. Boulder, Colo.: Lynne Rienner Publishers.

———. 1985b. "Toward a Reformulation of the Theory of Mutual Deterrence." *International Studies Quarterly* 29: 155–69.

———. 1986. "Recent Advances in Game Theory and Political Science." In Samuel Long, ed., *Annual Review of Political Science*. Norwood, N.J.: Ablex Publishing Corporation.

Index

189